HEALINGS, MIRACLES, AND SUPERNATURAL EXPERIENCES

HEALINGS, MIRACLES, AND SUPERNATURAL EXPERIENCES

HEALING 4 HAITI

Joan Hunter

DESTINY IMAGE® PUBLISHERS, INC.

P.O. Box 310, Shippensburg, PA 17257-0310

"Speaking to the Purposes of God for This Generation and for the Generations to Come."

This book and all other Destiny Image, Revival Press, MercyPlace, Fresh Bread, Destiny Image Fiction, and Treasure House books are available at Christian bookstores and distributors worldwide.

For a U.S. bookstore nearest you, call 1-800-722-6774.

For more information on foreign distributors, call 717-532-3040.

Reach us on the Internet: www.destinyimage.com.

ISBN 13 TP: 978-0-7684-3723-2
ISBN 13 HC: 978-0-7684-3724-9
ISBN 13 LP: 978-0-7684-3725-6
ISBN 13 Ebook: 978-0-7684-9013-8

For Worldwide Distribution, Printed in the U.S.A.

1 2 3 4 5 6 7 8 9 10 11 / 13 12 11 10

DEDICATION

This book is dedicated with great joy to those who have felt the tug to go to the mission field, were afraid to go, and went anyway—like most of the people in this book. It is dedicated with great gratitude and appreciation to those who *gave* sacrificially to this mission trip. It is also dedicated in faith to those who will read this book and decide to go somewhere, anywhere outside their comfort zone.

ACKNOWLEDGMENTS

Thank you, Doug Stringer, for the support and encouragement you have been to me personally and to this ministry through the years.

Thank you, Beth Carley, for your hours of work putting this book together. Thank you for serving my parents for over 22 years and for now serving with me.

Thank you, team, for going with me on the experience of a lifetime. It truly has changed us all forever.

A special thank you to my husband Kelley Murrell for the hours he put into editing and proofreading this book.

Last, but not least, thank you, Pastor Rene Joseph, for allowing us to come and join with you in Haiti. Thank you for all the work you did to make this happen.

CONTENTS

FOREWORD

Words are inadequate to describe the magnitude of human tragedy experienced by the Haitian people as a result of the 7.0 earthquake that hit their nation, January 12, 2010.

Many around the world watched the horror of their suffering depicted on various news reports, yet those reports paled in contrast to the indescribable realities of what the Haitian people actually suffered. Haiti, once known as the Pearl of the Caribbean, has become one of the most impoverished and corrupt nations on earth. Even before the January 12 earthquake, there were nearly half a million orphans. Now there are twice that many and hundreds of thousands of people who are still in desperate need. Billions of dollars of aid has been directed to Haiti from all over the world, yet with no proper infrastructure, no construction standards or systems in place, that money has been swallowed up by a deep hole.

Yet, in the midst of all this tragedy, there is a glimmer of hope and healing coming from God's people. The potential for a modern day transformation of a nation is set before us. Immediately following the earthquake, believers in Christ from around the globe put preaching into practice as they rallied together to become tangible expressions of Christ's love. Partnering together, leaders of various organizations put aside personal agendas to synchronize their efforts. Many of us were on daily conference calls to discuss the ongoing and ever-changing needs so that the shortest route of assistance could be mobilized as quickly as possible. Within hours and days, many of us were able to send teams to Haiti. Personally, I was able to take a team of leaders of organizations who dealt in four areas of basic human need: (1) food and nutrition, (2) medicine, (3) shelter and housing (short-term as well as long-term), and (4) trauma and counseling.

While seeing all the practical needs, many of us also recognized that any lasting transformation of Haiti must be both natural and spiritual. Local Haitian pastors and leaders, missions agencies, orphanages, and churches, though personally devastated, joined the list of unsung heroes as they sought to reach out to their people. I talked to directors of orphanages, pastors, and other leaders who themselves had experienced personal loss, including loved ones, yet their desire to win the lost became greater than their moments of pain. There are many genuine champions and heroes who may not get the recognition they deserve, but they continue to cast a vision of new possibilities and hope. I have had the privilege of encouraging many leaders and pastors in Haiti with the truth that it is God's plan to see their nation once again become the Pearl of the Caribbean. Pearls are a beautiful jewel, yet they come from great adversity and friction. Haiti has been through many difficulties, pain, and challenges, but it shall become a beautiful pearl among the nations once again.

There are still many needs, yet triumph is coming out of tragedy, and hope and healing are rising out of despair. Many champions of compassion and healing ministries are raising high the banner of faith, hope, and love. From healing explosions to persevering and transformational leadership gatherings, to ongoing humanitarian aid and tent outreaches, there is a renewed vision of hope going forth.

Two of the ministries bringing healing, both spiritually and physically, are Joan Hunter Ministries and Hunter Ministries, which are working alongside ministries such as Loving Hands Ministry, under the leadership of Pastor Rene Joseph. Joan Hunter Ministries and Hunter Ministries have ministered all over the world, bringing hope and healing to those in need. Alongside Loving Hands Ministry, just a few months after the Haiti earthquake, they held a healing explosion that touched hundreds of thousands. You will be encouraged to read the various life-changing testimonies in this book.

May you continue to pray for the destiny and healing of a nation and may you personally be encouraged to keep a vision of hope and healing in the midst of all that is being shaken. Keep your eyes fixed on the author and finisher of your faith, who for the joy set before Him endured the cross (see Heb. 12:2).

The whole earth groans with birth pangs.

For we know that the whole creation [earth] *groans and labors with birth pangs together until now. Not only that, but we also who have the first fruits of the Spirit, even we ourselves groan within ourselves, eagerly waiting for the adoption, the redemption of our body* (Romans 8:22-23 NKJV).

Doug Stringer
Founder and President
Somebody Cares America
Somebody Cares International
Houston, Texas

PREFACE

This book is a unique and precious treasure for many reasons.

First, it encapsulates the spiritual destinies and personal testimonies of many different individuals from a wide range of ages and geographical locations—a truck driver from Texas, a civil engineer from Oklahoma, a project manager from Ohio, a flight attendant from Georgia, and many others. Every team member shares his or her own unique story about the circumstances through which God brought them to Haiti and how He used them to minister healing to the people.

Second, this book comes at the beginning of a long-term involvement in Haitian ministry and relief efforts by Joan Hunter Ministries, Hunter Ministries, and many of the team members. Many of us will return to Haiti, and some of us will do so for many years. God released in our hearts a vision for Haiti that was far bigger than one mission trip.

Third, this book contains many moving stories of God's supernatural healing power. It chronicles a ministry of miracles and healings of every kind: blindness, deafness, trauma, hopelessness, lameness, epilepsy, and cancer, just to name a few. In a very real way, Haiti represents a window into God's redemptive plan for this new century. We believe that Haiti represents the whole world in a spiritual sense and that God intends to use His ministry to this small, impoverished nation as a sign of His greater Kingdom intentions until He returns.

He will mobilize the Church in the power of the Holy Spirit, not only to do compassion ministry and to plant churches, but also to demonstrate His power in triumph over the forces of wickedness in heavenly places. He wants to glorify Himself in one of the darkest and most desperate corners of the earth and thereby gain for Himself the reward He deserves for His own sufferings on the cross.

I am confident that God will use this book to stir your heart. As you read these stories, may you be drawn into mission work and given a hunger to see a broken world be healed and made whole.

> *God, mark us with grace and blessings! Smile!*
> *The whole country will see how You work, all the godless nations see how You save.*
> *God! Let Your people thank and enjoy You.*
> *Let all people thank and enjoy You.*
> *Let all far-flung people become happy and shout their happiness because*
> *You judge them fair and square, You tend the far-flung peoples.*
> *God! Let people thank and enjoy You.*
> *Let people thank and enjoy You.*
> *Earth, display your exuberance!*
> *You mark us with blessings, O God, our God.*
> *You mark us with blessings, O God.*
> *Earth's four corners—honor Him!* (Psalm 67 MSG)

Healing 4 Haiti

MARCH 30 - APRIL 6, 2010

INTRODUCTION

In 1983 I, Pastor Rene Joseph, had the privilege of being in one of Charles and Frances Hunter's services. It totally changed my life and how I pray for people. But before I share about my connection with the Hunters, let me provide some personal background.

My involvement in ministry began in 1978, when I first started planting churches in my homeland of Jeremie, in the southwest of Haiti. My pastor, Shoudelor, ordained me as a preacher when I was 19 years old. In 1981, a mission organization named Mission for Christ, based in Yukan, Oklahoma, invited me to work with them. They have over 30 churches in Haiti, and I became their secretary and translator. They also invited me to come to Oklahoma to finish my Bible degree. I decided to attend their Bible Institute, and while there, I met and married my wife, Dorentia. Our son was born there in 1985. Soon after, we moved to West Palm Beach, Florida, which is a lot closer to my home in Haiti. However, I felt called to return to Haiti; even though I started two churches in America, I always traveled to Haiti three to five times a year. Finally in 1986, Dorentia and I moved back to Haiti with our two kids, Ruben and Rachel. We went to the island of Lagonave, where I started seven churches in different places around the island.

In 1987, we rented a house at Delmas 31, in Port-au-Prince. I had had a dream in which God showed me that I needed to start a church at Delmas. He told me that, to prove that He was the one calling me, He would provide money to build a church and He would also provide transportation. We planted the church at Delmas 31 with 17 people, renting a room for $50 for six months. The church grew to 150 people, and we began looking for a bigger place to rent in less than six months. One day I found in my mailbox a check for $25,000 made out to me from the Bank of Connecticut. I still do not know who the donor was, but I know that the money was from God! We used it to build the church where we are currently running three services on Sundays.

One year after the church plant, a pastor from Fort Worth, Texas, Bob Nichols, bought me a new Jeep Isuzu Trooper. Truly God answered the promises He made to me! When we finished building our church, Pastor Tom Peter financed the first Bible institute for three years, enabling 27 men and women to graduate from it. Pastor Calvin Lyerla, of ACT2, also built me a pre-K through 6th grade school. Praise God for His provision!

We have gone out planting churches, schools, and clinics all over Haiti—in Jeremie, Cayes, the island of Lagonave, Port-Salut, Morne Sinai, Lacahonne, Anse Ainauld, Kinscoff, Archaier, and more. Now we have 34 churches, 7 schools, and 2 orphanages.

Dorentia and I have been married for 27 years and now have three children, Ruben Joseph, who is 25, Rachel Joseph, who is 24, and John Jacob Joseph, who is 19.

Now back to my connection with Joan Hunter Ministries.

After being so impacted by the ministry of Charles and Frances Hunter, when I heard that their daughter, Joan Hunter, was coming to Haiti, my heart leaped with joy. My heart is still so full of the blessings that resulted from the ministry of Joan Hunter and her team during the Easter weekend healing school and services that took place just a few months after the earthquake that tore our country apart. We gathered over 700 pastors from across Haiti. They all came hungry for a fresh word from the Lord as well as an impartation for healing ministry. Joan's personal testimony of the grace and healing of the Lord touched each one in a very special way.

There was such an excellent spirit that preceded the meetings and prevailed over each one. The miracles of healing and restoration poured down upon us like rain from Heaven. In all my years of ministry to the Haitian people, this was one of the most effective series of meetings and services I have seen. Joan Hunter is a servant of the Lord who has received a burden for the nation of Haiti. I look forward to a continued partnership with her for many years to come. I pray the Lord takes Joan Hunter Ministries to greater levels of anointing and prosperity so that others may be equipped to take the ministry of healing around the world for the glory of God.

CHAPTER 1

AN ARMY OF GOD GOES TO HAITI

BY JOAN HUNTER

On January 12, 2010, a magnitude 7 earthquake rocked Haiti. The epicenter of the quake was just 10 miles south of Haiti's capital, Port-au-Prince at a depth of 6.2 miles. It was the most powerful earthquake to hit in 200 years. The death toll was estimated to be at least 250,000 and about 1.5 million Haitians were displaced from their homes. Twenty percent of Port-au-Prince's buildings collapsed, and up to 80 percent of those still standing suffered serious damage and require repair or rebuilding.[1]

January 18, 2010, was a day like most days when I have the opportunity to be at home. It started out with my list of all the things I needed to do while I was at home. Getting my hair trimmed was the first item on that list.

Linda comes and cuts my hair about every six to eight weeks. I was looking forward to getting my haircut. When I sit down, she always asks me, "How do you want me to cut your hair?" I always tell her, "You decide. I make enough decisions!" It's our little joke. She does a great job and has cut my hair for over five years. But that day was different. I told her to trim the top and bangs, but leave the back long. I "felt" like I was supposed to let it grow for a season and wear my hair in a ponytail. I have had long hair for most of my adult life, but cut it short in 2000. This was the first time in my life I felt God leading me to let my hair grow. In that moment, as I sat listening to the still small voice of the Holy Spirit, my life and many others were changed forever.

The next day I went into the office and received a phone call from a man who used to work for my parents, Charles and Frances Hunter. His name is Pat McGuire. He had been talking with Bill Henderson, and they were trying to find someone to go to Haiti to train pastors and to lay hands on the sick—the only name that came up was Hunter!

He asked me if I would like to go, and knowing of the tragic circumstances caused by the earthquake that had struck just days earlier, I immediately said *yes!* Then I looked around the room to see who had answered for me. It sounded like my voice, but I knew it couldn't have been me! I am not the type to go to Haiti. I don't do well with sleeping in a sleeping bag on hard ground under a tent with hundreds of other women after a grueling day of relief work. I'm not into my husband sleeping in a different tent with a lot of other men and the port-a-potty being located far from my bed. And I love showers. But for some reason I was willing to give that up for nine days. This was not a normal decision for me, and I was quite surprised with myself.

We set the date for Easter weekend.

I hung up the phone and just sat there for a long time. It was as if I was slain in the Spirit while sitting in the chair and could not get up. When I finally got up, I called a staff meeting. I shared what God had told me about letting my hair grow and that I was going to Haiti. They began to cry, to rejoice, to laugh, and to clap. Some of my staff were speechless. Suddenly the power of God hit our room and burned a place for Haiti in our hearts that will last forever.

God Provides for the Trip

We started making plans that very day. This was to be the biggest endeavor that Joan Hunter Ministries or Hunter Ministries had ever attempted. We talked about going to Haiti to train 34 to 36 pastors and doing three nights of miracles at a church that held 1,000 people. I knew I could handle that.

We budgeted $10,000 for the event. This was a huge investment for us, but I knew we could do it. But we had one problem: Who was going to head it up? The office had too much to do and no experience in relief work. That was when God sent Eric Cummings to our office. One of our staff, Curtis, had previously worked with Eric on some relief projects. After talking with Eric, I hired him on the spot, and he hit the ground running. The mission plan grew bigger almost every day. I was told that we would have to do the services in a stadium. I said, "Fine," thinking that would only mean ministering to 50,000 to 100,000 people. It would be a stretch for the ministry, but I thought we could handle it.

The budget for the mission kept increasing every day. I thought, *OK, God, this is **Your** mission, not mine!* The response to our coming was so huge in Haiti that we had to move the gathering place for the healing crusade to an area outside the Presidential

Palace to accommodate hundreds of thousands or even a million people. The plan for the pastor's training was to bring the pastors in, train them, and send them back home. In order to do this, we had to pay their gas and food so they could come from all over the island. We also had to rent a facility to house the ministers, whose number had grown from 34 to 700.

Eric went down to Haiti and sent me an e-mail saying the projected budget on the ground would be around $100,000. Then shortly afterward, he sent me another e-mail saying, after recalculating the costs, the budget would actually be around $150,000. Further, he said we had to wire it by Friday, and it was already Wednesday. I was in Canada and had no affordable way to make international calls.

I sent an e-mail to the office and told them to write a check out for $2,500 to Somebody Cares, the ministry of Doug Stringer. It looked like we were going to need $250,000 for our Haiti mission (the $150,000 plus the cost of our flights and food expenses). I had learned what to do in such a situation. When God gives a vision, He makes a provision. When we have a need, God tells us to sow a financial seed in order to see that provision (see Luke 6:38).

Within 24 hours, I got a call. One person wanted to give $100,000 toward the trip, and we would be able to deposit it immediately. My husband, Kelley, drove across Houston and picked it up. He was excited that he was able to pray over it and put it in the bank. Then another call came in and another. Then checks started coming in the mail. Money was being transferred into the bank account from many sources. The trip itself cost over $250,000, but God met every need. To some ministries, this would be a small amount, but it was a huge step for us. This was more than what we normally banked in more than three months, which made the funding for the trip an even greater miracle.

God started bringing the people together from all over the U.S. and England to go with the team. God made sure that all of the fivefold ministries were represented on the team, apostle, prophet, pastor, teacher, and evangelist (see Eph. 4:11). Some of the team members had been in ministry for years; a few had only been in ministry for weeks. This was the first mission trip for many of the team members.

As the time for departure drew near, the excitement grew. I had to choose whether to walk in fear or walk in faith. God had taken this way beyond what I knew I could handle. He wanted to make sure it was *all* Him and none of me. We were very blessed in many ways, including total provision of the finances for this trip. We also had 50 bottles of hand sanitizer given to us by the manufacturer. I normally use it on the road, and it was great to give everyone his or her own bottle. I recommend this on a daily basis, especially on an overseas trip.

On the Ground

It was hotter than I had ever imagined in Haiti, and we had no rain during the days, even though it was the rainy season in Haiti. I will never complain about how hot Houston is again. I have never been so hot in my life. I remember saying, "I have sweat running down my scalp." This was a new experience for me; I normally don't sweat very much at all. We had very little relief from the heat and few showers. The water was so limited that it trickled when we had water and often was not there at all.

Over 40 people were staying in the mission house where we lodged. The mission house has three floors, and the women were on the third floor. At night, the men would gather downstairs and pray and worship God. We could hear them on the third floor. They were on the foundation of the house, and prayer was the foundation of this trip.

Incredible Breakthroughs Released to Pastors

The first day we ministered to over 550 pastors and leaders, teaching them how to minister healing. The excitement in their eyes and spirits was indescribable; they were so hungry. The first thing that I prayed against was the spirit of trauma—something they all needed badly. The longer I spoke, the more the heaviness lifted off them. Many of the pastors were healed, usually when they prayed for each other and themselves. The 36 team members also laid hands on the sick and saw them recover. Most of the team members saw more miracles that day than in their entire lives.

On the second day of training we had almost 700 pastors and leaders in attendance. They came from all over Haiti; some traveled over 24 hours to get to the meeting. I love ministering to hungry people. They were crying out for more and more of God and wanted to know everything they could about healing. Several doctors even came to learn and incorporate this ministry into their practices.

There was breakthrough in the area of word curses—for example, saying things like, "We will never get through this" or "We will never be able to rebuild Haiti." Then I ministered on godly restoration. I also spoke on finances and encouraged them to give to God and their churches like never before. I told them we were not going to receive an offering that day, but exhorted them to give to their churches. I told them to find something to give, even if it was only a button from their shirt. The power of God broke through, and people started bringing money up to the front. It was an awesome move of God because they received the revelation about giving from Him.

This reminded me of when my parents went to the Ukraine years ago. They had taken lots of clothing and things to give away.

While there, they taught a biblical view on prosperity. When they returned the following year, they discovered the people were dressed in nice clothing, with matching purses, hats, and jewelry. The change was so extreme that my parents wondered if they were actually in the Ukraine.

What really happened was that the Ukrainians got the message of the blessings of God in the area of finances—and that is what happened in Haiti too. We brought over 2,500 pounds of clothing, toys, and medical supplies with us. A spirit of giving broke out among the pastors, and many of them ran to the stage to give money. Many gave all they had, which added up to about a penny. They got the message, the spirit of poverty was broken off of them, and financial angels were released over Haiti. One pastor yelled out, "We want to pay your plane ticket when you come back!" They truly got the message. Most of the team was in tears because they had never seen the power of God move on people to give like that before. I expect that when we go back there will be a tremendous difference in their finances. Already they are seeing God's provision. Even during the service their cell phones started ringing (yes, they *all* have cell phones), and many were offered jobs. We then had an awesome anointing service. We lined up hundreds of the pastors around the meeting tents in a massive triangle. The line of people seemed several city blocks long.

Reaching the Hurting

Not only did we provide training for the pastors, but in the days following, during the mornings, we also visited some hospitals and orphanages and reached out to people in the streets. The experiences we had visiting the hospitals and orphanages will be burned in our hearts forever. Americans would never consider receiving medical help in these places, but they are all the Haitian people have. In the evenings we also held massive healing crusades.

Many people were healed. People often came up to us, placed our hands on them, and asked for prayer—in the hospitals, in the streets, and in the meetings. During the meetings, I prayed for about 40 individuals on the platform, and then we released the teams to pray for the masses. Blind eyes were healed and deaf ears were opened. Many of their testimonies are recorded in later chapters of this book. I prayed for a few each night after the teaching. After they were healed, they would pat their hearts and say "Jay-su." We had to stop praying for the sick at one point and just begin leading people to Jesus—hundreds of thousands welcomed Him in.

Each evening the crowds increased; word of the miracles was getting out and people were traveling miles to attend the meetings. I had to send an e-mail to my prayer partners, asking them to pray for increased wisdom for how to manage the growth. There were so many hurting people—we needed wisdom to know how to reach each one! Thankfully, the people in the crowds were excited to have all of us there, not just me. It didn't matter to them who prayed for them; they were healed anyway. Toward the end of the last night, I had the people all lay hands on their own bodies where they hurt; stomachs, heads, and backs were the main areas of pain. I prayed for their healings and then asked them to raise their hands when the pain had left. A sea of hands waved back at me. It was an incredible sight! On the last night of the healing crusade, so many were healed, delivered, and released from trauma that they didn't want it to end. They sang for hours, giving praises to God.

The meetings were all over the local news too. Many news stations interviewed me and recorded many of the miracles. Dutch, German, Haitian, and a few other radio and television personnel interviewed me. Several Haitian television and radio stations proclaimed this as the greatest thing that had happened to Haiti!

Truly the fruit that God reaped for His Kingdom during this short trip is incredible! Not only were so many healed and saved, but since we left, testimonies have begun coming in of new jobs and financial breakthrough as well. Further, each of the team members was forever changed by the experience. This points out once again the power of obedience! I wonder, had I chosen not to listen to God and had cut my hair, whether I would have received the call to go to Haiti. I don't know, but I do know that I don't want to be disobedient. When He spoke to me about my hair, not only was He preparing me to be able to wear my hair in a ponytail in the intense heat of Haiti, but He was also testing my willingness to obey. I felt Him say, "If I can trust you to listen about your hair, I can trust you to listen to Me in Haiti." Listen to the still small voice of the Holy Spirit, and He will lead and guide you into all He has for you! I am so thankful that I did. I left part of my heart in Haiti.

ENDNOTE

1. "Haiti Earthquake 2010: News, Photos, Engineering, and Maps" *MCEER* http://mceer.buffalo.edu/infoservice/disasters/Haiti-Earthquake-2010.asp#1 (accessed 6 June 2010).

CHAPTER 2

A NEW COMMISSION

BY KELLEY MURRELL

Husband of Joan Hunter and Vice President of Joan Hunter Ministries from Pinehurst, Texas

As Joan's husband I was quite surprised to hear that she had decided to go to Haiti. We hadn't discussed such a trip, and although Joan believes in disaster relief ministries, she doesn't normally go to those areas herself. But when a call came to go to Haiti, she knew immediately it was the right thing to do. At the time she made the decision, I was still working for a secular company, but it had always been our desire for me to quit my job and travel full-time with Joan.

The day after Joan made the decision to go to Haiti, I was let go from my job with a severance package. Joan called my change in employment status a graduation, not a termination, and I agreed. The run-up period before the trip was hectic, but God miraculously supplied the finances to cover the expenses, and He led a great group of people to join us.

Touring Haiti

Our first impression of Haiti came at the Port-au-Prince airport. The baggage claim area was utter chaos, reminding me of an enormous rugby scrum, and that experience turned out to be a true harbinger of things to come. Getting your luggage and finding your vehicle is a full contact sport in Haiti. We were met at the airport by Pastor Rene Joseph, our mission host, and several of his men who helped us get our luggage out of the airport and into our vehicles.

Most of the roads in Haiti are either broken, potholed concrete or washed-out, rock-filled dirt paths; goats and cows wander aimlessly on both. Driving in Haiti consists of a series of very close brushes with vehicles coming right at your vehicle from the opposite direction. I often found myself closing my eyes and holding my breath as we drove through the city, but by the end of our trip, I learned to relax, knowing we would not actually have an accident.

We stayed at Pastor Rene's mission house outside Port-au-Prince just past the U.S. consulate and the UN military depot. Some enterprising soul had put a mobile Domino's Pizza restaurant right near the two foreign bases and was doing a lot of business. The mission house is located on a hilltop and has water that is trucked in and held in a large plastic reservoir on the roof of the house. The water pressure was barely a trickle, and taking a shower required both resolve and great patience or a bucket, but we were well taken care of by Pastor Rene's people. The food they prepared for us was Creole in style and very tasty.

Meeting With the Pastors

We did two days of meetings with local pastors and preachers at one of the very few locations on the island that was not full of rubble or trash. It was green, lovely, and totally unlike most of the island, although we did not know it at the time. We were told that there were about 350 pastors and another 400 ministers at the meetings. It was a nice location with a small air-conditioned museum filled with artifacts from Haiti's past. We did these meetings under large tents outdoors.

Joan spoke through a translator on healing and finances. She always did demonstrations of healing after every teaching, and the faith level rose throughout the two days. I personally prayed for more than 20 men with a translator at one meeting, and as far as I could tell, all but one was healed. Large numbers of ministers and their wives were healed during these two days, but perhaps the most amazing moment came as a completely unplanned response to Joan's teaching on finances.

We had decided not to take up any offerings in Haiti, and the ministry paid all the traveling and other expenses of the ministers, some of whom had traveled for over 24 hours just to get there. However, after her message on prosperity, pastors spontaneously began coming to the front and throwing money, mostly small change, on the platform. I suppose anywhere in North America or Europe the small sums of money would not have seemed miraculous, but in Haiti it was incredible. A spirit of joy broke out because the pastors had a revelation that God would indeed respond and meet their financial needs. What joy! We have since received many testimonies of God's miraculous financial provision from Haiti.

On the second day Joan did an anointing service for all 700 people present. We lined everyone up along the triangular sidewalks that surrounded the tents, and Joan laid hands on everyone. The stillness and quiet expectancy of the people as they patiently waited for her to touch them was very moving indeed.

The grounds of the museum had some construction going on, and at times the workers on top of one of the roofs worshipped along with the ministers. One of our people even got some video footage of these men worshipping on the rooftop.

The Evening Crusades

The heat and humidity made doing large daytime meetings very difficult, so we had the crusade meetings at night in downtown Port-au-Prince. We did three large evening services on Easter weekend, and each night the crowds were bigger and more expectant than the night before. Hundreds of thousands of people stood for several hours each night dancing and singing with the worship team.

We had a good stage and sound/lighting system that Joan Hunter Ministries rented for the meetings so we could be clearly heard from a long distance over the crowd noise. The stage was across the street from the destroyed Presidential Palace and the people stood and worshipped God in the empty parking lots and the streets between the tent communities, which were everywhere. After long worship periods, Joan preached relatively short messages of about 20-25 minutes and then started praying for the sick on stage. Each night as the people on stage were healed, the level of excitement in the crowd rose.

Joan preached messages of hope for a new Haiti and spoke some general prayers over the crowd. You could literally see waves of people being touched by God in the huge crowds as she prayed away trauma and survivor's guilt. God healed people in large numbers as Joan prayed, but the 36 team members were also laying hands on the sick and seeing amazing results. As team members prayed, many blind eyes and deaf ears opened, the lame walked, and Haitians were healed of all kinds of diseases and conditions. A number of demonized individuals were delivered who had been involved in voodoo. One young girl in the middle of an epileptic seizure was also healed.

At the first evening meeting, some of the crowd got a little impatient and started pushing against the barricades to get to the stage. We soon realized it was best to release the ministry team members to pray for the sick at the same time Joan prayed for them on stage to prevent a panic in the crowd. One evening the people got so excited that Joan had to stop praying for the sick to allow the pastor to give a simple presentation of the Gospel.

People wanted to get saved at that very moment, and they did not want to wait!

Pastor June, a friend of Pastor Rene Joseph and the man we hope will be the next president of Haiti, gave a short Gospel message and led hundreds of thousands in the sinner's prayer. It was an incredible experience just to be there and watch so many people get saved at one time. I held my breath at one point while they were praying the sinner's prayer because it was as if the whole world stood still as the Holy Spirit descended on them *en masse* in one moment in time. Eternity met time and seemed to swallow it up, at least for a brief moment.

Visiting the Orphans and Sick

We also visited one hospital and two orphanages during our trip. The hospital would not be used for anything other than possibly a warehouse in the U.S.—that was how primitive it was. In the new mothers' ward, newborns lay next to their mothers, crowded into a small room with no lights or fans in the oppressive heat. One new mother tried to give her baby away to one of the ladies to take back to America. We prayed over the new moms and their babies. We also toured around the rest of the hospital praying for the sick.

The first orphanage we visited was in the country. It usually takes care of about 200 orphans and provides them with something to eat and a place to sleep. However, when we drove up in a big yellow school bus, hundreds of other children swarmed onto the orphanage grounds looking for something to eat or some gift. We tried to give away some clothes and toys, but that almost sparked a riot so we had to give everything to Pastor Rene to distribute after we left.

We prayed over the grounds and inspected a cement block factory they are trying to build. The kids were fed a corn meal mush, which was cooked over an open wood fire in large metal bowls, and they were very glad to get it. Some sneaked back into the line to get second helpings. You don't see many overweight Haitians.

The second orphanage we visited was a home that sheltered children from birth to four years of age. It was a very nice place, and the children were well cared for. We prayed for the kids and went back to the mission house.

Haiti in Our Future

As we prepared to return to the U.S., we all longed to take long, hot showers and to sit in our air conditioned homes. While in America, the two-thirds world can seem like an unpleasant dream that you hope you never experience, but God loves those people as much as He loves us.

Once back in Houston, Texas, Joan and I only stayed 12 hours before we had to leave for Phoenix, Arizona, for her daughter's wedding. We stayed in Arizona until Sunday and then returned to Houston. We left the following Friday morning to do 16 meetings in 5 churches in 10 days in Indiana and Kentucky. We were exhausted after the Haitian trip, but God strengthened us, and we have seen incredible blessings on the ministry since we returned. We know now that God desires for this ministry to return to Haiti often. We have received prophetic words that God desires to use Joan to spark a revival in that broken land. We know it is a commitment that will last for years because God wants Joan Hunter Ministries to be involved in the rebuilding of that island with a new spirit for His glory.

CHAPTER 3

GAME ON

By Eric Cummings

*Missions/Event Coordinator for Joan Hunter Ministries
from Houston, Texas*

I had been out of work for two months after leaving a previous job as construction manager with a local non-profit that was doing hurricane relief work in homes in the Houston area. I was blessed to have time off with my wife and newborn baby girl, but money was getting a little tight, and we had gone through most of our savings.

I made contact with a friend named Curtis Wilke, intending to have him pass along my résumé to someone he might know for possible employment. Little did I know what God had in store! God had already spoken to Joan, and the vision of going to Haiti had been birthed. Shortly after that, Curtis spoke to Joan and told her about some of my past experience with missions and organizing both mission trips and volunteers. Not long after, on February 2, Joan asked me to come on board and to put together a trip to Haiti. Praise God I had a job again!

Making Plans

Originally Joan told me they wanted to take 200 volunteers down to Haiti to minister to the pastors, leaders, and people of Haiti. I said out loud, "Two hundred, no problem!" On the inside I was thinking, *Are you kidding me?* My next thought was, *Not my will, Father, but Yours be done.* As it turned out, this number shrunk to 36, which was much more manageable.

My friend Curtis soon made another connection for me, this time with Pastor Calvin, a minister in Florida who had partnered with a pastor in Haiti for about 17 years. This man, Pastor Rene Joseph, had recently led a three-day fasting and prayer event in Port-au-Prince, the final day of which culminated in a one million person gathering outside of the collapsed Presidential Palace in downtown Port-au-Prince. I shared our vision with Pastor Calvin, and he made the connection for me with Pastor Rene, who was thrilled to have us come. After just a few weeks of planning, I found myself in Haiti.

I met Pastor Rene at the incredibly chaotic airport in Port-au-Prince. I was a little unnerved by the masses of unorganized people, but fortunately, despite the confusion, he picked me out of the crowd and introduced me to Haiti. I spent three days with Pastor Rene, and though we had never met before, it felt like we had been friends for a long time. In those three days, we planned the entire trip, including accommodations at the mission house and both venues for the training and the crusades.

During that time, God also gave me a vision of Joan Hunter Ministries holding our crusades at the exact location of Pastor Rene's earlier million person prayer event. At that exact location each year, all of the voodoo priests from around Haiti would gather over Easter weekend for their services and blood sacrifices. But we were called here to reclaim the country and its people for Daddy God and His purposes. God opened the doors for us, and we were able to hold our healing crusade adjacent to the collapsed Presidential Palace.

"No Problem"

I flew down early with another team member to do a last bit of recon and to double-check all of the arrangements. It was just as I had expected—no problems. Whenever I would ask Pastor Rene a question or make a request, that was always his response, "Eric, this is *no problem*." I love meeting people of like mind who want to do nothing but help people and build the Kingdom of God. Pastor Rene truly is such a man and working with him was both a pleasure and an honor.

Three days later, we met our group at the airport. It was like stepping into a cage with 200 other people for a game of full-contact baggage claim. Let me do the math for you. There were a total of 136 suitcases plus various other bags. Everyone was trying to identify their bags and keep track of their carry-ons in an area the size of a Starbucks. We survived—no problem! After piling everybody's luggage into an open bed truck and the people into a school bus, we were off to the mission house.

The mission house was a blessing from God, even though it had no air conditioning and no hot water (or water pressure) and you could not drink the tap water. However, there were beds for each one of us with actual pillows and sheets. We also had six bathrooms, each with a commode and a shower. We were also blessed to have two awesome home-cooked Haitian meals a day provided for us. Originally we expected to sleep in tents with bed rolls, cooking our own food, using portable showers, and sharing a hole in the ground for a bathroom. We were willing to do whatever it took to answer the call of God! So even though quarters were close, and we learned to be more patient than I think some of us knew we could be, we were thankful to be indoors and on a mission—that kept us focused.

Only a few of us actually knew each other, but it was like we were family from the very start. We were 36 people sold out for God and invading Haiti for the same reason—to bring glory to God while bringing the healing power and love of Jesus Christ to a hurting people and lost nation.

Teaching at the Museum

The first two days we held the pastors' training at the Sugar Cane Museum; it was incredible. The pastors were eager to see God heal and to learn how to heal the sick. They had heard what God wanted to do, and they wanted to be part of it. By the middle of the first day, approximately 500 pastors and leaders had arrived. We spent about an hour and half in worship; the Holy Spirit was flowing, and everyone was absorbing Joan's teaching. Day two was even better, with approximately 700 to 800 pastors and leaders in attendance. Even some very influential leaders from around the country attended, including Pastor June Chavannes, who has been a pastoral leader in Haiti for decades and is in line to be the next president of Haiti.

There is no doubt that God has His hand on this country now and is ready to bring it back to Himself! And He is touching and equipping the Church leaders in powerful ways. My favorite part about both days was when the team was able to pray for the pastors and watch them receive healing by the power of Jesus Christ. Not only did they experience healing, but they also got the message that they too could lay hands on the sick and watch them get healed.

After the pastors' training event was over, we had an opportunity to visit a local open air market so everybody could take a little bit of Haiti home. They had many handcrafted items, especially globes of the world.

Healing in the Streets

The next three nights at the healing crusade were indescribable. The first night God brought in about 200,000 people, filling the streets around the Presidential Palace. Praise and worship went on for at least two hours, and the excitement of the crowd was tangible. Joan had a word for the people of Haiti. "You are not alone. God loves you. God wants to bless you. God wants you to prosper. God wants to take you to the next level of relationship with Him. God is ready to build a New Haiti and wants your help."

The number of salvations, healings, and miracles experienced that night was in the tens of thousands. It was a late night by the time we made the bus ride back to the house, but nobody wanted to do anything but give glory to God and rejoice in the presence of the Lord.

The following day we made a stop at a local hospital to lay hands on the sick. This was quite an eye opener for all of us. Most of us were not prepared to see what condition the people were in, let alone the condition of the hospital itself. I noticed that jacks held the ceilings and walls in place so they would not collapse! The sanitary conditions were terrible because there was not enough help, sporadic electricity, not enough supplies, and too many people. But God had sent us there to bring prayer and hope to His people.

The second night of the crusade was more powerful than the first. By that I mean that the presence of the Holy Spirit and the sheer number of people who came had greatly increased. About 300,000 to 400,000 people were in the streets before the night was over. The number of salvations, rededications, healings, and deliverances also went up dramatically.

Day three was Resurrection Sunday. We were blessed to see four or five local churches come together corporately to celebrate Resurrection Sunday—a day of decreeing and declaring, of reclaiming the streets, the land, and the people. God is good! That evening's miracle service was the most incredible of all the services and ministry that had taken place while we were in Haiti. The praise and worship was fantastic. God had saved the best for last. Over 600,000 people filled the streets and every nook and cranny as far as the eye could see.

The number of people who came to experience God for the first time was overwhelming. The healings and miracles were too numerous to mention, but blind eyes opened, the deaf ears could hear, and the lame could walk. Everything I'd seen while running volunteer camps for disaster relief after Hurricanes Katrina and Ike paled in comparison to what I saw in Haiti. I thought I'd seen God move before, but I was wrong.

Firsthand Healing Encounters

God allowed me to experience two separate incidents that will be in my mind and on my heart for the rest of my life.

On the second night I was in the crowd around the stage when someone handed a young girl to me over the barricade. She was limp from head to toe. Her eyes had rolled back in her head, and she appeared to be near death. The Holy Spirit told me to get her up on stage. I rushed her over to the stage and handed her over to another team member, Brian Guillory. I told him what was going on and he took her to Joan. She was instantly healed from the top of her head to the bottom of her feet and walked off the stage with her mother. Glory to God! She could have been prayed over off stage and received healing, but God wanted her up on stage so that thousands of people could see Him heal her.

The last night there was a huge call for salvation. Thousands of people gave their lives to the Lord. I was down in front of the stage praying for people, and God led me to one lady in particular, a large woman on crutches, standing by herself and singing with everybody else. I passed by and asked her (through an interpreter) if she would like prayer. She said yes. Before praying for the injury on her ankle (an open sore that she had suffered in the earthquake and that had not healed up yet), I asked her if she knew Jesus as her Savior. The answer was no, and I had the honor of leading her to the saving knowledge of Jesus Christ as her personal Savior and Lord. I then prayed for her ankle and knew it would be healed. Toward the end of the night, the entire stage broke into spontaneous celebration, dancing, singing, and rejoicing in what God had done. As I joined them on stage, I noticed that the lady whom I had prayed for was up on stage dancing and singing too, but without her crutches. Instead, Pastor Rene was dancing around with them above his head.

Feeding the Children

On Monday we visited the site of Pastor Rene's future orphanage and a community he started further north up the coast, near a town called Archaie. What an awesome time we had feeding all the children. Most of them were either orphaned by the earthquake or in a single parent home because of it. They are very poor and have very little to eat. We used the money that team members had brought from their churches or organizations to buy the corn meal to feed about 500 kids. We also got to love on them and play with them.

Pastor Rene's ministry, Loving Hands Ministry of Haiti, also has a school that sponsored children can attend. We learned that for only $24 a month we could sponsor a child, providing him or her with school tuition, a uniform, daily food at school and some to take home, and a connection for the parents to better themselves. This really impacted me. My wife Cyndi and I have a six-month-old baby girl, Casey Annabelle. She is the most precious and spoiled thing in the world and has a world of opportunity ahead of her here in the U.S. These children don't. That is why we decided to sponsor a little boy in Haiti.

We then went to another piece of property that Pastor Rene has right on the Caribbean, the future site for his missions retreat house. We played and swam in the ocean for a couple of hours, relaxing from the intensity of our trip and enjoying the beauty of Haiti.

On the last day we stopped by another orphanage, one supported by Doug Stringer and Somebody Cares America, to pray for the babies and children. Some of the babies were orphaned, some were from single parent homes, and others were just abandoned by their parents after the quake because they could no longer take care of them. It was an awesome time of ministry. Afterward, we returned to the house, got our things together, and headed for the airport. Farewell Haiti! We all made it home safely and with changed hearts and a new fire for the mission of spreading the healing power and love of Christ around the world.

Home Again, but Changed

Since I returned to the U.S., God has allowed me to step out further in faith and trust what He wants to do. The Haiti trip inspired all of us at Joan Hunter Ministries, and we felt the Lord leading us to expand our vision—so we scheduled mission trips to five countries (Mexico, Ireland, Haiti, Costa Rica, and El Salvador) for the remainder of 2010. If that doesn't sound like fun (and a faith-stretching adventure), I don't know what does.

Those who know me know that my favorite phrase is, "Game on!" Now that doesn't mean that I think that all of this is just a game. It means that God wants us to approach Him with excitement, expectation, and childlike faith. What child do you know who does not have fun at almost everything? Let's get out there and get in the Kingdom Game that God is coaching. He is looking for eager, excited children whom He can show how to win. We are called to be diligent about our Father's business, walk in the ways of His Son, carry the Good News of the Gospel of Jesus Christ to the whole earth, and have a great time doing it!

CHAPTER 4

THE OTHER SIDE OF THE ISLAND

BY CURTIS WILKE

Secretary/Treasurer of Joan Hunter Ministries and Treasurer of Hunter Ministries from Texas City, Texas

Twenty-two years ago I went on my first mission trip to Puerto Rico. On that first mission trip, a seed was planted in my heart for missions, disaster relief, and the people of the nations. Though I didn't know it at the time, it was the first step toward my trip to Haiti. Five years later on a mission trip to the Dominican Republic (which is on the same island as Haiti), I received a wake-up call from God. He showed me where I had been and where I was going. I found myself surrounded by people living in houses built with four poles, a tin roof, and cardboard or tin sides, but despite the conditions, I saw happiness, cleanliness, and spiritual freedom in their eyes and actions.

The core of the mission trip to the Dominican Republic was building a library for the seminary compound. We experienced building with less than the bare essentials. We hand-mixed concrete and sand on the ground and then scooped the mixture into five gallon buckets. We then hoisted them ten feet into the air to pour the second floor of the building. There was no lack of willing local labor to work in this grueling environment. Unemployment is high, so there is no need to find efficiencies in the workplace. The more people who can be used to work on the project, the better, and the cost of their labor is a small percentage of the overall cost of projects. The reality of seeing what most of the world has and the abundance of blessings that we take for granted in America shook me to the core. The average Dominican at the time had a third grade education. This really hit home as I had completed three and a half years of college before leaving to build an empire in the marketplace.

On our last day in the Dominican Republic, we ventured into a marketplace loaded with handcrafted treasures, sculptures, and paintings. The paintings were the key. Paintings in the Dominican Republic have lots of color, light, and scenic views. But they also had Haitian paintings, which were much darker. I could see the oppression and heaviness that rested on the Haitian people in their art, and I knew then that I would return to see the other side of the island.

Following that, in a season of transition, I sold the first of several business ventures and returned to college to finish what I had started. Driven by the desire to finish and add Spanish to my vocabulary, I completed a new degree program, much to my parents' delight. After that, I was personally involved in many disaster relief programs, including the cleanup of Florida after Hurricane Andrew and sending medical clinics and containers to Granada and Indonesia. I also participated in sending food, water, and various supplies to Mexico and New Orleans and East Texas after hurricanes.

Then on January 12, 2010, a major earthquake devastated Port-au-Prince, Haiti. It did not take long for a call to help Haiti to come to Joan Hunter Ministries and Joan personally. My spirit was already stirred and shaken by the reports of what had happened in Haiti. Inside I was already programmed to respond to this major catastrophe and overjoyed to learn that Joan had answered God's call to go and bring hope to His people in Haiti. I was now part of a team committed to going and training small groups of pastors living in Haiti.

First, God brought a co-worker from the past into my path. Eric was looking for something to do. He had worked in a key position with me in building and delivering medical clinics to Indonesia after the tsunami. I met with him and got his résumé for Joan. I also met with a couple of men in Denver who wanted to go to Haiti to help the pastors. During sessions they decided that "we need a Hunter to go and impart healing in Haiti." Representing the Hunter healing legacy, Joan had picked up the torch several years ago and recently received her parents' healing mantle in addition to her own healing gift.

At the meeting in Denver I heard Joan once again say, "I will go," and the power of God hit all of us. Joan said it again, "I will go," and God opened the gate as I turned to Joan and said, "Now I know why Eric handed me his résumé. We need to have Eric head up Healing4Haiti." The call to offer him the job was placed moments later.

How do you know when God is in charge of a plan? You clearly see that it is God-sized, and you see no possible way of doing it by yourself! In this case, what started as a plan for a small group of pastors to receive teaching and impartation for healing grew to a call to the nation and over 700 pastors and leaders being trained to help their people. Healing and miracles service venues went from expectations of 500 to 1,000 at the church, to a soccer stadium size of 100,000, to a God-sized crowd of over one million participants over Easter weekend.

Miracles started happening right away to both encourage us and confirm that this was His plan. The ministry committed to go, and plans started lining up key people and finances. After a couple weeks into this mission, I still did not have contact information on Pastor Rene or confirmation that Bill had a plan in place. Finally I got a call from Bill's assistant and a number for Pastor Calvin in Florida. I anxiously called Pastor Calvin to get some information about Pastor Rene and what we could do to help. I shared with Pastor Calvin our vision to go to Haiti Easter weekend. He was surprised that we would pick this time on such short notice because the group that had planned to come over Easter had canceled about an hour before my phone call! We also received some more information concerning a prophetic word sent to the president of Haiti. The next day Eric and I had a conference.

Circling the Wagons

Have you ever noticed the feeling you get when a big change or a challenge is about to come your way? You get a knowing in your spirit that it is time to circle the wagons and focus on what is coming over the horizon. That was our welcome to Haiti. There was a huge battle erupting in the spirit because this airplane was coming to deliver equipment and spiritual tools to God's leaders in the spiritual battle for Haiti. As the airplane was circling in the natural, we were circling our wagons in the spirit. With each passing circle we made while waiting to land, I saw a glimpse of the evidence of the destructive power of the earthquake. Buildings reduced to rubble were scattered here and there, but the fields full of tents were signs of what we were entering into.

"Good afternoon and welcome to our tropical island of Haiti" was not the sound or scene that welcomed us to the airport. Making our way off the plane to the baggage claim area, we saw the broken airport support equipment and damaged buildings. All of our flight's luggage was transferred by hand to a big open room inside the terminal and piled in a huge pile for the owners to identify and claim. It was interesting to see the reactions of the people as they realized that A/C and electricity had disappeared from their environment for the next eight days. With our seasoned support team and lots of willing hands, our luggage was gathered and cleared for transportation to Pastor Rene's mission home.

Immediately after clearing customs we were thronged with offers to help and to sell us souvenirs and items for personal use, like sunglasses. All along the way there were street vendors doing whatever they could to exchange their goods for our money. Knowing that we had come to help, we were all cautioned not to give money or things to the people because we would all become targets.

We saw tents and shacks along the roadside. As we looked into the people's eyes, we could see a reflection of the trauma and destruction they had experienced. When we caught them off guard, they were often staring off into space without hope or direction. It is a nation of lost, confused people who feel helpless to change their own lives. The people know there is food, water, and help streaming into their country, but they aren't getting much help personally. *Where do I go to sleep? How do I fill this big empty void in my heart? Where are the rest of my friends and family? Who cares?* Knowing that we were in a bus coming to help deliver answers made our spirits alive and ready for the call we were answering!

The Original Mission

Equipping the local and national pastors was our first priority. During the praise and worship the overflow of the Spirit touched workers on the rooftops and people attending other events, and it drew the attention of the local and international media to witness God's love in action. During the training you could feel the leaders soaking up every word. As different ailments were called out, people came up front for prayer. One by one, God healed their bodies when Joan ministered "pray teaches," showing the leaders how to pray for different pains and sicknesses. This brought many of the pastors to their feet because they were witnessing things they had prayed and believed for, but not seen.

We were hot and tired at the end of the first day of training, but the fire of the Spirit energized the team. Arriving back at the mission house, we were greeted with a variety of rice, bean, and chicken recipes throughout our stay. It is amazing how much water you can consume and how soon you learn to drink liquids at a full range of temperatures!

The men found fellowship and prayer time in the evening to be the crowning jewel for a day spent building the Kingdom. Each night we gathered to pray, share needs, and watch God move our hearts. Music, prophecy, and words of knowledge came as Joseph led the men each night. The unity of the team grew and strengthened each day.

On the second day of the leadership seminar the number of attendees grew. After more teaching and healing it was time for impartation and the laying on of hands. It was an awesome sight to see hundreds of leaders line up around the park to receive an impartation from God through Joan. Each one was touched and activated by God to change this nation at a time of catastrophic disaster. I could see the fingerprints of God as He works to turn and woo a nation back to Himself.

A stranglehold of the enemy was also broken. Joan shared the testimony of her parents going to a very impoverished area of the Ukraine. Frances taught the Kingdom principle of sowing and reaping, tithes and offerings, and the activation of spiritual laws. When they returned a year later with suitcases of clothes and articles to bless the people, they thought they were at the wrong place. People who had been walking were now driving; the homeless now had homes; and nice clothes replaced the rags they were wearing. This came about all as a result of obedience to God in giving.

One of the parameters of our mission to Haiti included that the ministry was not to receive any offerings in the services, but the Holy Spirit is in charge, and at the end of Joan's teaching a spontaneous offering move happened, and every person charged forward to give offerings to the Lord, breaking the poverty spirit off the people.

Here's the result! In a country shaken and battered by an earthquake, almost everyone carries a cell phone even though they have lost everything else. As soon as the spirit of poverty was broken through their activation of biblical principles, people's phones began ringing in the service. They were receiving job offers in a country where the whole economy and job market had come to a virtual standstill. The testimonies are still coming in about the positive change in finances and living conditions because people were obedient to the Word and broke the spirit of poverty.

After the impartation and distribution of certificates, the team was released to pray for any of the leaders who wanted prayer. Healing lines developed around each of the team members as God used them, and hundreds of people were healed. I believe every word spoken was planted in fertile ground and that this harvest will continue for years to come.

Paulette and Geoffery, who joined the team from Phoenix, Arizona, work for Patricia King and XP Media. On Thursday night God released Paulette to prophesy over anyone on the team who wanted a word from God. I was blessed and honored to record each prophetic word. It was an amazing and intimate time with the Lord as each team member sat and received direction, impartation, and confirmation. This experience created memories for a lifetime. For me, it was an activation and confirmation of things that I received in a dream from childhood. I believe God lets us know His will for us by giving us many different confirmations.

The Toolbox Anointing

Now that we had accomplished our original goal to train and activate the Haitian pastors in healing, it was time to focus on possessing the land for the Lord. It was Good Friday, and God had made it clear to me that we had to have new tools for the assignment that we were on. In my case, I refer to it as the toolbox anointing. I am going to share this in a way that may activate this anointing in your life right now. You will have to read this and then close your eyes and remember what you read and ask the Lord for your new Kingdom tools and toolbox.

The toolbox anointing relates to a supernatural experience I had in Florida. After Joan taught a healing school at Ignited Church in Lakeland, Florida, we attended Sunday morning services the next day. At the service, Pastor Stephen Strader invited Joan's team to come forward and receive from the Lord. As Pastor Stephen prayed over the team, one by one, I could feel the tangible presence of the Lord. I was standing there with my arms stretched out in total surrender to the Lord when the Spirit directed me to lower my arms and stretch them forward with my palms up to receive. It was as if someone was to hand you a very large package. It was at that time that everything changed. I sensed the presence of at least two angels. I did not see them in the natural, but I perceived them in the spirit. The first one carried a large, heavy toolbox with drawers over to me and placed it in my outstretched hands. I held it and waited as a second angel came to me with a long rectangular box that could hold a very large sword. I then set the toolbox down and received the long rectangular box.

As I stood there with the two packages, I asked, "Who's to receive them?" The answer I heard was Pastor Stephen. At this point the anointing was flowing, and I shared with Joan what had happened and the need to deliver the toolboxes to the pastor. The delivery was divinely delayed until we joined him and his team for lunch. It was on the way from the church to the restaurant that obedience to deliver the packages activated the greater assignment to deliver toolboxes to leaders around the world

Now back to Friday morning in Haiti. We gathered for prayer before going out Friday to a hospital. The toolbox anointing was there after the prayer, and toolboxes were delivered to each of the team members. This was a timely delivery as we all used some of our new tools at the hospital and throughout the day. *This is a moment to pause and clear your heart and mind. It is your time to close your eyes and with a clear heart stretch out your arms and hands to receive your tools and your toolbox to run the race and finish strong in Jesus' name.*

At the hospital, my team consisted of Phil, Bione, Richard, and myself. We were sent to the surgery ward for men. While waiting to go in, I reached out to a couple visiting their aunt. Since most of the people we encountered spoke French, I was surprised when this couple spoke English. It was a divine encounter for him because he had been crying out to God to send someone who would speak into his life and situation. We talked briefly and I introduced him to Pastor Phil. God stepped in, and they were gone to their own divine appointment for the next 45 minutes.

Richard, Bione, and I went on in to pray for the men, their friends, and other visitors. Richard prayed for a man who had lost his leg, and I prayed for another who had serious damage to his legs and upper body. Bione prayed for another one who had been injured during the earthquake and others who needed surgery for internal problems. They all received healing for trauma, and the countenance of their faces showed relief and hope instead of pain and despair. As we rounded the last bed before going out, the man who had been missing a leg was now getting dressed to go home. The miracle was that he was putting his legs (not leg) into his pants! Thank You, Jesus!

Going Deeper Into the City

We moved around the city in a retired school bus. The roads were marginal at best and non-existent at worst. Some of the potholes we dodged would swallow a person on a bike or small scooter. The larger open areas were covered with tents and makeshift houses built from tin and scrap. The streets were lined with entrepreneurs selling handmade items, food, beverages, and trinkets made in China. Every time we slowed down, the venders would quickly come to the sides of the bus hoping to catch someone's interest and make a sale.

We went into areas where damaged structures and rubble extended as far as you could see. I was reminded of going into the Ninth Ward of New Orleans after Hurricane Katrina. Haiti had been shaken to its core. Buildings had been leveled, dreams were crushed, and lives were extinguished in a few tragic minutes. The damage the quake left behind was more than physical; it was also mental and spiritual.

We could not look in any direction without seeing displaced people, crumbled buildings, or trash and debris as we proceeded to our destination across from the Presidential Palace. The magnitude of the destruction was overwhelming. Our location was in the same area voodoo witch doctors made annual blood sacrifices, until now. We started Good Friday decreeing and declaring the nation of Haiti for God. This set the stage in the natural for a supernatural outpouring of the Holy Spirit.

As praise and worship cleared the atmosphere, thousands came to see what was happening in the area known for government power and corruption, blood sacrifices, and homeless people living on the streets. Joan started to pray for the sick one at a time in groups of 20. As the miracles and healings happened, the crowd grew restless and anxious for a touch of God. We released the team to start praying for people they could reach inside the safety zone. Everywhere I went with the video camera, the window of the supernatural opened. Healings and miracles happened every time the team members prayed. Hearing was restored, blind eyes opened, deaf mutes spoke, and hearts were restored in Jesus' name!

The level of expectation grew as we prepared for Saturday and Easter Sunday. Every night we prayed for the rain to stay away and for mild breezy weather to reign throughout the day. God answered our prayers with a breeze and light showers to cool and cleanse the land at night!

Saturday came with the excitement of a Christmas morning as a child runs to open gifts. Our gift was the people who had heard about the healings and miracles from the last night and came to see for themselves. The crowd was building, and Geoff and I climbed up several hundred feet in a nearby tower to take pictures and videos. The people looked like ants coming out of the woodwork to hear the voice of God and receive their healing. The crowd stretched for blocks in all directions from the platform.

The wooing of the Spirit drew people from all circumstances and religious beliefs to the platform.

The praise and worship went higher and higher as they sang "pick up a rock and throw it at the devil." Another song referred to running all the demonic influences out of the country and into the sea. Another one said that evil has no place in their country anymore.

That night we brought people from the front and the back of the platform to help ease anxiety in the people who hoped to have Joan pray for them. Again we saw backs and shoulders healed, trauma leaving, and bodies restored. One young lady came forward with a broken left arm. It was obvious that it needed to be set, and she had been without medical attention since the quake three months earlier. Joan prayed and the lady tested it. It was better, but still painful. Joan prayed again and the arm looked straight and had a lot less pain. She then went to the side of the platform while Joan prayed for others.

Later the lady emerged from the side of the platform raising her arms and praising God. She then confirmed that the Lord had healed her arm, the pain was gone, and she had full mobility restored to her body. The crowd went wild shouting and clapping praise to God! All around the platform, the team spread out praying for people. Some had interpreters and some did not because the number needing prayer was so great. As I walked through the throngs of people wanting prayer, I would film the miracles taking place and then stop and pray for those tugging on my hand. One after another, they would communicate by putting their hands on where it hurt so I would know where to place mine. It was amazing to see God heal them one after another even though we did not understand each other.

A very special treat awaited us when we returned to our mission home: Domino's pizza! We were all excited to see, smell, and eat a familiar American food. There were lots of smiles and spirited conversation as we ate and shared some of the miracles that happened that night.

The mission house was built out of solid concrete and rebar, including the roof. This allowed us to go upon the roof of the house and get a great aerial view of the valley and Port-au-Prince. We took lots of pictures and prayed over the city. In the middle of our corporate prayer, I looked up and saw a heart-shaped cloud confirming the love we have for the people of Haiti.

On Sunday morning we put on our spiritual armor, knowing the significance of Easter and the restoration of Haiti. Like a team of race horses, we were pawing in the spirit with great expectation. The morning service consisted of praise and worship teams from the many churches connected to Pastor Rene. It was a great time for the youth to praise God for bringing them through the earthquake. By 11 o'clock Pastor Rene delivered his Easter message, and it was getting too hot for the people to stand in the sun. We took a mini tour of the city and went to our first air conditioned building since leaving the airport. It gave us a break from the heat as we ate and prepared for the evening service.

The man in charge of security for the Haitian president also led our security team. He cleared the way for us to go over to the Presidential Palace for a group picture and watched over our team as we walked back to the platform.

That night praise and worship filled the air, bringing Heaven to earth for a moment of time. Angelic hosts sang in the spirit to the King of kings and the Lord of lords. The chanting of "pick up a rock and throw it at the devil" filled the air. Expectation exploded into determination. Joan had to stop praying for individuals and pray for the masses because of the size of the crowds. Then Joan commanded the spirit of trauma to leave the people. She prayed for people with back, knee, and shoulder problems. Thousands were healed at the same time. God used the miraculous to loose a hunger for salvation in the crowd. Joan had to stop praying for the sick because the lost wanted Jesus in their hearts immediately. Tens of thousands became Christians at one time.

This was the greatest miracle! Waves of healing continued well into the evening. As I kept moving around in our safe zone taking pictures and praying for people, the time flew by. As I was making my way through the crowd and taking single photos with another camera, a young girl kept tugging on my arm. By this time we were all used to the near endless lines of people needing prayer, but this one was different. She would not stop tugging on me because she wanted me to pray for her grandmother. (I later learned that Eric had already led the grandmother to salvation—seed time and harvest in action!)

She led me to her grandmother who was hunched over on a set of crutches and barely able to move. Her body was racked with pain, and she was crying out for prayer. I learned what was wrong through her granddaughter and an interpreter. I put my hands on her neck, shoulders, knees, ankles, feet, and back while I prayed for the pain to go and new parts to replace the old ones. We thanked Jesus and then I asked her to walk without the crutches. She did! I knew God wanted to use this miracle so I got Pastor Rene's attention with the crutches and told him we should have her come up on the platform to share her testimony. He waved us up and the crowd witnessed the miracle as she started to dance on the platform without her crutches! This raised the praise and worship to a higher level, and the crowd jumped and praised God. Thank You, Jesus!

Meeting the Children

Monday came in a little on the quiet side after the awesome miracles over Easter weekend. It was time for us to see Pastor Rene's vision for his 80-acre compound and to feed the children at the orphanage and school. The compound has a school, dining hall, and cooking facilities, and right behind the compound there was a small cement block pouring facility. Barry and I observed and hand-tested a couple of the blocks to verify the lack of quality control and the need for establishing testing standards for the cement blocks. This is essential for the vision to work because these cement blocks are used to build small efficient homes on the property. The last thing the people need is structural failure from the building materials.

The children were very friendly toward the team and bonded with us instantly. As I was walking and taking pictures, they all wanted their pictures taken. They loved to see their images on the camera screen. Several little ones held my hand as we walked around the compound. When the sweet corn porridge was ready, the dinner bell rang and the children streamed into the dining hall. They sat squirming in their seats waiting for the serving pans filled with what would be their only meal that day. It was very humbling to watch as some of the littlest children would make sure others got enough to eat before turning their dish back in.

Our last stop allowed us to see and feel the beautiful blue water of the bay on a lot housing a future mission home. The mission home is for pastoral retreats and refreshing. The view and water were beautiful. A large island across the way waits for visionary developers to turn it into a vacation center.

Tuesday morning was the final day and our last outing before going back home. We got to see the orphans at the Somebody Cares home. The ladies and guys enjoyed the opportunity to meet the kids and see the needs of this facility. Most of the children here will go back home to their parents after things settle down or when they are healthy enough to go back home. Most of us started thinking about how we could make a difference in Haiti.

The trip back to the mission house got a little exciting as we got close to our departure time and our bus ran out of fuel. One of the worse things to do to a diesel engine is run out of fuel or put contaminated fuel in the fuel system. We were about to experience both! There were no service stations in sight. We had to find fuel and starting fluid fast and hope the battery lasted. Our driver brought fuel back in plastic liter jugs sold in the open air in the median of the highway! The fuel was probably contaminated, and we needed the now smoking hot battery to stay strong.

As I stepped out of the safety of the interior of the bus into the traffic-clogged streets, I remembered Joan's request that we seed $91.00 into a ministry for our safety. I had seeded mine shortly before we left Texas, and our protecting angels shielded us from any harm as we worked to get the bus running again. We soon got the bus started and back on the road. Thank You, Jesus and the angels that surrounded us! A few more exciting moments happened between the bus and everyone getting on the plane, but our mission was a huge success.

Longing to Return

We rediscovered the modern world when we returned. Running water, A/C, cold drinks, hot showers, nice roads, green grass—welcome home! But what a longing we have to go back and help Pastor Rene and the people of Haiti. We hope to go back before the presidential election in November.

New contacts and connections happen daily as we plan our return. Work has begun on water and sewer projects that will bring safe drinking water to Port-au-Prince and surrounding areas. A water filtration unit is being designed for the mission house and soon-to-be-built dormitories plus a bottling system to help bring in additional finances. It may be possible to have cement trucks and a batch plant donated. Additional teaching materials are being gathered for our return. Stateside adoption is being looked into to help place the 200,000 plus orphans into loving homes.

CHAPTER 5

THE BLESSING IN SERVING

BY KRISTI STRAND

*Nurse in the recovery room of a surgery center in
Plano, Texas*

A couple years ago I attended an ordination with Charles, Frances, and Joan Hunter. As a nurse, I've felt called to the healing ministry for a while. But through my time at the ordination, God confirmed and strengthened it in me in a whole new way. I wanted to see people healed, not only through medicine, but also through supernatural miracles.

After the earthquake hit Haiti, a couple of the doctors I work with went to Haiti to assist with surgeries such as amputations, setting broken bones, and wound closures. I had been asking God for a while to send me on a mission trip where we would operate in signs, wonders, and healing miracles. After what happened in Haiti, I started crying out to God with even greater passion, asking Him to help me find a ministry that would go and bring His supernatural healing power to the people of Haiti. God answers prayer. Not long after, I happened to go to Joan Hunter's website and discovered my opportunity to go to Haiti. I applied and was accepted!

God had to work many miracles in my job and circumstances to make the trip possible—and He came through in amazing ways! At my job, we make our work schedules two months ahead. Our March schedule had already been completed, but I went to my boss, who is a Christian, and told her I really wanted to go on this trip. She responded with, "You have to go." She allowed me to change my schedule and use my vacation time. I was also scheduled to be on call during many of the days of this trip, but the nurses I work with graciously took all my calls.

As a single mother, I needed to find somewhere for my daughter to stay. Usually her best friend's family is out of town during Easter, but this year they weren't and she was able to stay with them while I was gone. Lastly, I was also asking God for the funds for this trip. I gave an offering to the Lord, and that very day a nurse at work gave me a check and two others gave me cash. It was incredible to watch the Lord provide in so many ways.

Blessings at Every Turn

We came to give and serve, yet we received so much. The lessons I learned from my team members and the Haitian believers have forever changed me. It is incredible how, in the midst of giving, we received so much back!

One of the main things I wanted to bring was much-needed medical supplies, so I asked God to help me decide what to bring and to help me get it. Both of the surgery centers I work for donated gloves, sutures, medicines, and all sorts of medical supplies. When the doctor who works with Pastor Rene saw the medical supplies we brought he said, "God knew these were the things I have really needed." I was so blessed to see God's provision and guidance!

Even though we were the ones who had come to teach and pray for the sick, the Haitian people really touched my heart. Their hope and trust in God was incredible. Their praise and worship was so beautiful, powerful, and deep—an expression of their love, passion, and gratitude for God and what He has done. After everything they have been through, they could have been angry and bitter, but they were praising the Lord.

The team of people God brought together was also such a blessing to me. Each person came with joy, love, and great expectation to see and experience God more. Their stories of how God was working in their lives were very inspiring to me. I have never spent a week with such incredible men and women of God who each day demonstrated how to truly walk out what they believe and have fun doing it! I kept thinking, *What an awesome way to spend my vacation time!* He called each of us to Haiti to bring hope and to demonstrate His incredible miracles. We were a team of ordinary people, some pastors and ministers, some mothers, fathers, and housewives with secular jobs.

The crusades were more of a blessing than I could have imagined. Each night they grew more powerful and more people would come with expectation to see God move—and He did. I believe this faith and expectation released such an atmosphere for the miraculous that thousands were healed, delivered, set free, and saved. By the power of God, there were many healing miracles through the hands of everyday people. I cannot put into words what an honor and privilege it was to be used of God like that. It was an answer to prayer and a confirmation of His Word to see these miracles.

In Second Chronicles 7:14 it says, *"If My people, who are called by My name, will humble themselves and pray and seek My face and turn from their wicked ways, then will I hear from heaven and will forgive their sin and will heal their land"* (NIV). As this verse depicts, when the people on our team and many Haitian believers participated in three days of fasting and prayer, God truly showed up.

A Willing Vessel

Through my experience in Haiti, God, Jesus, the Holy Spirit, and His Word have become more alive to me than ever before. Not only was I blessed, but as I shared the testimony of our trip later, many others also found hope for their own miracles. I believe it has inspired others to pursue miracles here at home and in other nations. God is real. He is the same yesterday, today, and forever. And He wants to see His people whole, healed, and delivered. God is who He says He is and will do what He says He will do. I am so thankful to have been a part of what He did during our trip to Haiti!

We did what the Bible says; we laid hands on the sick and saw them recover; we cast out devils and saw the captives set free and saved. We saw thousands of people healed of every sickness, disease, and infirmity. God wants to use all of us. All we have to do is say, "Yes, Lord, here I am a willing vessel; use me." It's so exciting to see hope and peace restored to people's lives, to watch them experience the love of God. God can use each one of us in this way—it's our destiny, and it's exciting!

CHAPTER 6

STEPPING OUT, BREAKING FORWARD

BY DARON MOSLEY

Senior Estimator/Project Manager from Ashville, Ohio

When we first heard that Joan was looking for volunteers to join her team to Haiti—and that we had two to three weeks to decide whether we wanted to go—we began praying about it. I felt led to go, but was not so sure about my wife, Kim, going with me. It seemed pretty dangerous; at that point we thought we might be sleeping in tents. It also seemed unlikely that, without the funding to pay for most of our fare, either of us would be able to go. Then God put us on the fast track. We found out that we had to not only complete all of the paperwork, but also come up with the $600 each in our own funds and book the flights to join the team so that we would all be together entering Haiti—all in less than 48 hours.

Jumping Hurdles

My biggest question was, "Why, God, if You wanted us to go, are we not getting money from Joan's funding?" We were being tested to make the decision as a leap of faith! My next obstacle was my concern for what we might see and the living conditions that Kim might have to endure. I had been through most everything during my time in the military—no showers or toilets and sometimes uncertainty regarding availability of food and drinking water, or even a place to use the toilet.

We got a quick response from our spiritual mentors, Mike and Cindy Teagarden. They said we should both go or neither of us should go. Fair enough. By the time we heard that from Mike and Cindy, I had heard the same in my heart from God. With that settled, Kim and I began to pray about Haiti. We asked the Lord to show us clearly and undeniably if we should not go.

In the night, I awoke concerned about Kim's passport. We had not yet changed her name to Mosley since our honeymoon. I did not think it would be that serious; we'd just take our marriage license along like we did on our honeymoon cruise. But according to the government, it was imperative and a potential stopper. But God! The short of it is, we had her passport processed and returned just one day before we boarded the plane for Haiti. Praise God! No worries!

Then I just needed to get an OK from my new boss for another week of paid vacation. I had just recently used two weeks off for our honeymoon. I did not expect any resistance, but I was wrong! He thought I was nuts for going to Haiti, and he could not justify paying me another week of vacation. We had our first riff, but I was already committed to going, and I would not let the prospect of a week without pay plus travel expenses get in the way. My boss stood his ground about the pay, but did agree to pay me for two of the seven work days that I missed. Not another word was said about the riff. After we returned, I shared some photos, but he is still shaking his head as to why I would have wanted to go.

To top it all off, at work we began working on a three million dollar bid just three days before we were leaving for Haiti. I would have less than one full day back from Haiti to pull the bid together. No pressure! I made one brief appeal to abort the project to my counterpart on the project, but to no avail. I am certain he thought I was nuts for going too. But I had no time for boo hoos. I got to work and trusted God that He would give me all the pieces before and after I returned from Haiti. And He did.

Encountering Devastation

As we left for Haiti, I really had no real idea what I might contribute overall. I just knew for sure that I was "called" to be there. Soon, I would find out.

Haiti was really hot and dry. The quarters were way better than I expected and so was the food. But the heat was tough, and we had no air conditioning—but considering that millions of Haitians live in the streets, it was not so hard. I even managed a trickle of a shower each day, not just one every three days. Thank You, Jesus!

The drives to and from the training sessions at the museum near the center of Port-au-Prince were just a taste of the devastation we encountered. There are no pictures that can fully describe what I saw every time we stepped into that bus. The destruction, the chaos, the traffic, so many people in the streets, so many sitting or standing and staring into space—it moved my soul.

Where are they working? How are they surviving? The people have scarce, polluted community watering holes, no electricity, and few toilets. Thousands live in shanties made of sheet metal and tarps or tents with no floors. I could hardly imagine lying down in the gravel and dust just to sleep a few hours in the darkness before rising again at dawn to start another day. Men sweep up huge piles of brick and rubble with shovels (not backhoes) and push wheel barrows from dawn until dark. Others saw off pieces of rebar and drag them down the street to scrap yards tied to a back of a motorcycle! Women walk miles carrying heavy buckets of water on their heads. Everyone is scrounging and peddling anything they can get their hands on to survive.

If nothing else, I will never forget how good I have it here at home in America.

Something else that really caught my attention was that every residence and every place of business, not just in the city, but even on the outskirts of town, was fortified with barbed razor wire and broken glass stuck in the mortar to keep intruders from climbing the walls. I wondered why such poor people would spend so much of their meager resources to protect themselves, and from what? What are they all afraid of—each other, evil spirits, the government? Most of us have no idea what it is like to live in that kind of fear. Can you imagine living in that kind of constant danger?

Translating Words

The healing school for the Haitian pastors was an awesome gathering in a huge tent outside at the museum. The Haitians all dressed in their Sunday best for the training meetings, most of the men and boys wearing suits and ties and the women wearing long dresses. I hung my head thinking of how put out I felt at not being allowed to wear my shorts in that blistering heat. Sorry, Lord! Those Haitians, young and old, take the opportunity for Spirit-filled worship and learning about the Lord to a level that we American Christians should aspire to! We take so much for granted.

It was late in the second day at the healing school when I got my first real glimpse of why I was there. A Haitian pastor was sitting on the steps of a building in front of us. The school had been dismissed for the day, and we were waiting for the bus to pick us up. His name was François. He was probably a little older than I am, mid-40s, just sitting there deeply engrossed in his Bible. He also had a red pen and a notebook. I introduced myself, and he quickly began asking me to help him interpret specific words in his Bible. He spoke pretty good English, but struggled with many of our English words that change in meaning according to their context.

We spent the next half hour going through several chapters of the book of Psalms. He would underline the words and then make notes on his notebook, with accent marks to help him remember the meaning of each word. He was eager to learn more, and his patience was refreshing. He was so happy that he could understand the words that had been unclear. I did my best to explain the meaning of the Scriptures. It was a divine appointment for me.

I met him again the next day as we walked to the bus. We managed to decipher a couple pages of his Bible along the way. His thirst for the Scripture blew me away! I could not find him a Bible in Creole that he asked for, but I encouraged him to come to the Healing Explosion the next day (Good Friday) in Port-au-Prince. He said he would be there. I did not see him again until the end of the Easter Sunday morning service. We were heading to the bus again, and he came to me, his Bible in hand, with a pen and his notebook. We went over several more words as I climbed on the bus. I cannot imagine the impact of his ministry in Haiti, but with his thirst and perseverance, I have a feeling it will be awesome. I hope to meet him again one day.

Seeing the Miraculous

Good Friday morning, Curtis met with all of us in the main lobby of the house. He was praying for each of us individually and handing over to us spiritual "tools" that God had told him to pass on to others. I was blown away when he told me I already knew a little about the tools the Lord was handing over to me. I was receiving powerful weapons for spiritual battle, not just swords, but precision tools that would have very specific tasks. Whoa!

Later that night, just before the events were getting started, I felt the Lord tell me to walk the perimeter of the barriers speaking in tongues. I made two laps around the perimeter, having no idea what I was speaking. I am fairly new to the gifts of the Spirit. Before we'd left for the trip, I'd had a vision. I was not sure if I was inventing it in my head, but I could not get it out of my head. I told my wife Kim and several others before we left for Haiti—I'd seen a person walking toward me with his arm stretched out toward me. His arm was broken, and then it was healed!

Now it was show time. It felt a little like running out onto the football field just before the big game. We were given the word to go and pray for the people. The security guards were trying to keep it orderly and were letting a line of those needing prayer inside the barricades in front of the stage.

There were no interpreters behind us as Kim and I walked toward the barrier in the middle of the stage. I looked around to see where we could find someone to interpret. I looked back, and a man appeared in front of me walking directly toward me with his hand stretched out. His wrist was badly swollen, and his arm was wrapped in gauze.

I looked back for Kim behind me and standing right beside me was an interpreter. I have no idea where he came from. We found out the man had fractured his arm and wrist. I was nearly overwhelmed with the appearance of my vision. It was like I had been standing right there at a previous time. I prayed for his arm to be fully restored and the bones mended in Jesus' name. He could move his fingers a little, but I could tell he was still in pain. The interpreter discovered he was better, but could not twist his wrist and still had much pain. I prayed again for the muscles, ligaments, and tendons to be restored and the swelling to go down.

Again I saw a vision of this man being healed, so I could not stop until his miracle had manifested. Somehow I knew his arm would be restored! I told him to thank Jesus for his healing and to start clenching his fingers and hand. You could see the strength coming back each time he clenched his fist. He then grabbed my hand and squeezed it very hard. He couldn't clench his fist before, let alone squeeze my hand like that. We all gave glory to God for his healing, and he went off into the crowd pumping his hand high over his head. Hallelujah!!

This was the first of many miracles and healings we experienced in the next days. Wow. Glory to God! The openness and desperate condition of those who needed prayer was humbling. Though it was not possible to pray for every one of the thousands and thousands who needed prayer, I believe all who came would have gladly embraced our prayers.

Indeed, the tools God gave us we put to use immediately. We only had 10 to 15 minutes to pray that first night at the end of the service. And the anointing was powerful! Kim and I prayed for ten people, three men wanting to be set free from madness and seven women, whom I thought had bloating from parasites or worms. Praise God they all got healed!

Easter Sunday, we arrived a little late and the crowd had already swallowed the space in front of the grandstand. I did not get to walk the perimeter this time. We were released almost immediately to pray for all those who needed prayer. There were hundreds of Haitian people hanging on and climbing through the fence, many starving for prayer and clearly desperate for healing. Those images may never be erased from my memory. It was an awesome exchange to be used as the Lord's healing hand for those in need.

It was awesome as well to watch and join the Haitians singing and dancing in worship like there was no tomorrow. They could go on for hours and hours worshipping, and they had us doing the same even though we had little idea what we were singing. The way they all worshipped, young and old, is even more amazing considering how little they had and how much they had lost. You could see hope being restored in their eyes.

I praise God for enabling me to be a small part of that experience! I somehow know it will not be the last I see of Haiti. I believe that entire nation is on the way to full restoration! Hallelujah!

Redefining "Comfort Zone"

At the end of the trip, I returned to my comfort zone. I use that phrase cautiously, for what I once knew as my comfort zone is being transformed daily. Having survived a near death experience a few years ago, I have been on an incredible journey of spiritual growth that was accelerated in Haiti. I am so thankful that Jesus is teaching me humility, compassion, and love.

While in Haiti, I believe we were able to plant many good seeds and that none of us know what will grow out of that explosion of faith and obedience, not only in Haiti, but also in our own lives. For me personally, I know I received an anointing during the trip that I am only beginning to understand. It is one thing to say Christ is in me and yet another to release and watch God's miracles and healings manifest through my own hands. How incredible it is to feel the love of Christ flowing through my hands and my voice to those who desire so much to receive and believe. To God's glory, I was touched even more than all the people who were prayed for and healed. I got a taste of what I imagine is coming as we approach Christ's return to the earth.

Participating with Joan's team was awesome, and I think it was just the beginning step for Haiti and other nations all over the world. It is my prayer and desire to grow and reach out to people here at home, most of whom have no idea how good they have it, even while they complain and worry about their own surroundings. The walls of self-pity and self-righteousness are so high.

It amazes me how much more difficult life is for those among us who are suffering, yet they resist even the smallest gesture of prayer from a friend or co-worker. The battle is great to win souls like in Haiti, but God has shown me that it is greatest right here in our own circles of friends, family, and co-workers. It has begun to stretch my comfort zone to the max. I find myself urged to walk up to someone I never would have even noticed before and to speak to his or her needs. *Wow! How risky is that?* But what am I risking, really? How can I go on missing those opportunities? I pray the Lord will continue to work in my heart to shape mine to be like His everywhere I go!

CHAPTER 7

WAKE-UP CALL

BY KIM MOSLEY

Specialist Systems Analyst from Ashland, Ohio

You've just read my husband's version of our trip to Haiti. Allow me to share my perspective with you as well. As Daron said, when we heard about the mission trip to Haiti, we both felt drawn to be a part. We prayed about it for several weeks and really never had a "no" in the Spirit, but we never had a "go" either. Though we were concerned about finances and about leaving Daron's 12-year-old son at home after just getting custody of him, we couldn't shake the idea of the trip, and both of us felt we should go.

On the financial side, I was not expecting a bonus or a raise for the 2009 year. I work for an insurance company, and there were lots of losses and the economy was still doing poorly. Over 200 people lost their jobs in my department alone. God spared me as I was moved to five different positions. A week prior to the deadline of getting all the paperwork in for the trip to Haiti, I was called in for my annual review. Not only did I receive a substantial raise, but I also received a bonus. The bonus was just enough to cover our airline tickets to Haiti.

There were many other miracles that took place as God gave us favor with our vaccinations, provided short lines at BMV's, opened the door for Daron's parents to come to stay with his son, and helped us get time off from work. We do not know why God would choose to allow us to be a part of this trip, but we are honored and humbled that He made the way. As a newlywed couple, we would never have dreamed we would become a part of a trip of this magnitude.

As Isaiah 6:8 says, *"...Here am I. Send me"* (NIV). And He does because of Calvary!

Beyond Imagination

Words could never express what I was about to witness as I stepped off of the plane in Haiti. Only God knew what lay ahead for me and the other 35 members of our team—experiences of both incredible devastation and miraculous power. I've been to other countries and traveled quite a bit, but I'd never seen such devastation and poverty before. As we worked our way through the crowded airport, where the temperature was at least 100, we all were excited to see God's hand work before us and through us, even though most of us had no idea what we were getting into.

The part of our trip that stands out most in my mind is the three nights of the healing crusade. I never dreamed I would ever see so many people longing to worship God. It was 90 degrees, and they had suits on, but they worshiped for two or three hours! It was the time of my life—truly electrifying to be among all of the Haitian people worshiping God! I didn't know what they were saying, but I could *feel* what they were saying! The power of God increased as the evening wore on.

When it came time to pray for people, the barricades weren't able to hold people back! They were climbing through the fences to receive prayer. Little kids just longed for a touch. As the lines grew for people needing prayer, we took them one by one.

One instance that stood out the most to me was a little nine-year-old boy. His mom and grandma brought him. He had been very sick about three years prior, and during the sickness he had quit talking. He hadn't spoken since his sickness. I prayed for about half an hour with this young boy, and he just stared blankly at me. I couldn't let him go though. I kept telling him to say, "Thank You, Jesus." He just continued to stare. I had his mom and grandma clap and praise the Lord with me, saying, "Thank You, Jesus." Then we would go back to the young boy and try to get him to say it. I held my hand on his chest and gave it one more try. I said, "Say, thank You, Jesus," and I felt a vibration. I said, *"Go ahead! Say it! Thank You, Jesus!"* Then, it happened; he said it! A soft and gentle, "Thank You, Jesus," came forth out of that little mouth and his mom and grandma were ecstatic! I'm so thankful I never gave up and that God gave me the perseverance to see him through to his healing!

I witnessed many people with bad knees who could barely walk eventually bend and stoop on them with no pain! I saw many healed of headaches. I prayed for many people who were full of parasites from the drinking water. I prayed for the chains of poverty to be lifted off of everyone and for complete restoration of their digestive systems. I knew in my heart that if they could be free from parasites and poverty, they would have the means to get clean water. I was overwhelmed by how open and receptive the Haitian people were to healing. They believed and so did I. I know this is only the beginning for the country of Haiti and that this country will be fully restored!

Drinking Water

My life will never be the same after this trip. Since I've returned home, I have learned not to take things for granted, especially water. I came to work the next day, and as I walked to the ice machine with my bottle, I stopped and thanked God that I had the ability to fill my jug up with ice and fresh, clean water. Sometimes it takes a wake-up call from God, in a trip like this, to make us really understand the needs that exist around the world and how petty ours may be in comparison.

My heart tells me that I will return to Haiti again. I expect to see a new Haiti upon my return. As they move the rubble brick by brick, I see new bricks being laid—brick by brick. I believe this country will be a prosperous country, not to mention a country that attracts tourism via *many* cruise ships! I have a newfound love for the Haitian people, and my life is forever changed as a result of this trip. Thank You, Jesus.

CHAPTER 8

CHANGED ON THE INSIDE

BY BARRY PYLES

*Civil Engineer with the Army Corps of Engineers in
Tulsa, Oklahoma*

As I watched the news after the Haiti earthquake, I saw Marines handing out Meals Ready To Eat (MREs) to Haitian people. The Holy Spirit spoke to me in my spirit that "Christians will be feeding hungry people, not like you see the Marines are doing, but like Jesus did when He fed the 4,000 and 5,000."

I was so excited that the Holy Spirit had talked to me and that Christians would be feeding the hungry. I thought of many scenarios where Christians would be sent into countries to feed the people. The people would eat and then listen to the Gospel preached to them. They would surely respond to the Gospel if their bellies were full. This could even bring Muslims to Christ. I looked up the Bible verse where Jesus fed the 5,000 (see Matt. 14:16-21). Jesus wanted His apostles to feed the 5,000, but they did not have the faith. They said it would take a week's wages to feed all the people. The same goes for us today. If we don't have the faith to allow God to feed the hungry through us, then it won't happen. I told a friend of mine about what the Holy Spirit had told me, and he said that God wouldn't have told me unless He wanted me to be a part of it. *Wow!*

A couple of days went by and I received an e-mail from Joan Hunter informing me that she was going to Haiti and was looking for volunteers. I thought to myself, *Maybe God will work through us to feed the hungry.* When I got Joan's e-mail, I was already fully funded to go because a few months prior I had taken retirement funds out to pay off debt. God was definitely telling me to go, so I signed up. I realized later that God wanted me to go for another purpose as well.

God changed me on the inside while I was in Haiti, though it wasn't apparent to me until I came home. Things that were important to me before are not as important to me anymore. He gave me a love for the Haitian people and for the mission team members. He also gave me a desire to fulfill the Great Commission and to lay hands on the sick so they would recover.

Laying Hands on the Sick

During the three healing services, it seemed that the Lord healed anyone I laid hands on. I prayed for about 10 people the first night (it was cut short because of a security problem), at least 20 the second night, and at least 50 on the last night. God's anointing was flowing through me. All the other team members were experiencing the same thing.

Most Haitians were physically traumatized from the earthquake and were experiencing headaches, pain in the abdomen, and lower back. It was rather difficult at first trying to understand the Haitian people's problems, but the interpreters were invaluable to the team. It wasn't long before the Haitian people would just point to the place that was hurting. I would pray for that part, and Jesus would heal them! Praise You, Jesus!

One old woman whom I prayed for complained of back pain; as I prayed for her lower back, God instantly healed it. She complained about not being able to see well. I laid my hands on her again and prayed. God again instantly healed her eyes. She walked around with her hands up praising Jesus.

I prayed for many Haitians who had traumatic symptoms. After I prayed for one Haitian man who had traumatic symptoms, and God healed him, he told me about a voodoo disease on his feet. I noticed there was a pool of water under him. He took his socks off and showed me his feet. His feet were dripping wet, and both feet had large sores and water was oozing out. I commanded the voodoo spirit to come out of him and asked the Lord to let His healing flow and restore both feet. The man went away praising and thanking God for his healing.

I prayed for an eight-year old child who had refused to eat ever since the earthquake. The child's stomach was round and hard. I bound and cast off the spirits of trauma and fear in Jesus' name. I prayed that God would give the child a creative miracle, a new digestive tract and stomach in Jesus' name. I couldn't immediately verify this miracle, but in my spirit I knew Jesus had healed this little boy. I also prayed for a pregnant lady who had traumatic symptoms and was concerned about her baby. God healed her symptoms and she left praising Jesus.

"Merci, Jesus!"

When I approached Haitians to pray for them, usually their eyes were filled with pain and defeat. After I prayed for them, God healed and filled them with His love and joy. They would leave with a peaceful and happy look, saying, "Merci, Jesus!"

The Haitian praise and worship during the healing services was amazing. Even though they were singing in French Creole, which I can't understand, I could feel the presence of God. God was blessing the 36 Americans at the same time that He was healing and blessing the Haitian people. They were singing and dancing before the Lord for two to three hours. I wanted to stay another week so we could lay hands on as many Haitians as possible, but even seven days wouldn't be enough to touch all 1.1 million Haitians who attended all three services.

During a praise service, another team member, Debra Hoskins, showed me a photo she took of me with an orb over me. She told me it was an orb, or angel, which are described in Ezekiel 1. When I came home and looked at more of her photos, I saw that there were hundreds and hundreds of orbs all around the Haitian people and the 36 American volunteers. The orbs were more numerous during the praise and worship services. I even found a couple of orphanage photos with orbs. God takes care of His kids! The photo below shows a gigantic orb that appeared over the platform before the healing services started. Nobody could see the orbs, but we could definitely feel God's presence. It appears this orb, or angel, being approximately six-feet in diameter, was rather high in the angel command structure because it was the largest orb that showed up in any of the photos.

Taking It Home

God has blessed me so much as a result of this trip. He has given me a love for the Haitian people and the Haiti team. I have a desire to do whatever the Lord throws at me. The Lord has put on my heart to seek out and lay hands on the sick and brokenhearted.

It started at the Houston airport while I was waiting for my connect flight to Tulsa. As I sat down, the Holy Spirit radar went off. I knew the Lord wanted me to pray for somebody, but I didn't know who. I looked around, and when an old man with his left leg propped up came into my sight, the Holy Spirit alarm went off. I asked the Holy Spirit, "Is this the guy You want me to pray for?"

He said a resounding, *"Yes!"* After thinking about it a few minutes, I walked over, not knowing what to say, and said, "The Holy Spirit asked me to pray for you. What do you want me to pray for?"

He said, "Yes, I do need prayer." He explained that he was recovering from cancer and the chemotherapy treatments were causing problems with his lymph system and swelling his left leg. It felt better to him when the leg was elevated. He also told me that he had back pain and had a disease in his eye, which caused him to only see to the side.

I prayed for his legs, his pain in his back, and his eyes. I left without seeing an instant miracle, but I felt in my spirit that God was working on him. I asked the Holy Spirit for a sign. Sometime later the man lowered his leg and was rubbing it. Praise God!

Since I've been back home, I have prayed for all of my family, friends, and whomever God brings across my path. I recently had a request from a friend of mine to lay hands on and pray for the friend's eight-year-old grandson who is deaf. He can hear a little with the aid of a hearing device implanted in his skull. I am pestering my family all the time asking if their backs or shoulders are out of alignment or if they have pain. I am determined not to miss out on opportunities to pray for people as I have done in the past.

Back in the 1980s I attended a Church of Christ and was praying for a friend who needed surgery. I heard a voice say, "Touch him!" I looked up to see who was talking to me. Nobody was there so I continued to pray. I heard that same voice say with more resolve, "Touch him!" This continued, but finally I decided not to pray for this man. When I decided in my mind not to lay hands on this man, the Holy Spirit convicted me. I'll never miss an opportunity like that again.

Spreading the Word

Since I've been back home, I have had the opportunity to be on a panel discussion at John Brown University in a Construction Management class to discuss construction quality control in the private industry. During my briefing, I found myself giving Haiti a plug, and I told them that Haiti needs construction managers just like them in the worst way to help rebuild their country.

After the panel discussion was over, two students came up and told me they were going to Haiti in December 2010 as a part of Franklin Graham's Samaritan's Purse ministry, which brings over student construction managers to help with the rebuilding. God is bringing the people and resources to Haiti to rebuild it!

During a construction class I teach with the Corps of Engineers, I also took the opportunity to tell the contractors about my adventures in Haiti. I told them how Haiti needs quality control contractors to ensure construction is achieved for new facilities.

Every chance I get, I tell people how Haiti needs support in rebuilding the country. Hopefully sometime soon, God will provide me the funds to go back to Haiti to help Pastor Rene Joseph build his orphanage. Whatever the opportunities, I know I will be eagerly volunteering for mission trips such as the Haiti trip because I want to be there when God feeds the multitudes through His Church. Glory be to God forever and ever.

CHAPTER 9

REBUILDING THE RUBBLE

BY PAULETTE REED

Evangelist, Founder and President of Paraclete Ministries,
Prophet from the Nation to the Nations

When the very first promo for this trip popped in my inbox, I felt a prompting to go to Haiti. I just held it in my heart. Then I was at a meeting and I said to a woman I barely know, "I feel a nudge to go to Haiti on a short-term mission trip."

She immediately said, "I'll pay for your ticket!" She went on to explain that she had received an inheritance, and the Holy Spirit had told her He would let her know where the tithe was to go. It was awesome! Never in my life has this happened. I even had enough left to purchase a video camera. Extreme Prophetic also helped with expenses from our missions funds.

Since I'd been so blessed financially, I went to Savor's to get some clothes and hiking boots to leave in Haiti. I prayed about the boots and found a nice pair for $6.99. They are brand-new. When I googled the brand, I found out that they are Mephisto Warrior shoes that usually cost $380.00! Amazing! God truly made a way for me!

The God of Miracles

During our time in Haiti, the part that impacted me the most was praying for people to be healed during the three-night crusade. As I was meeting people in the prayer line, I would say to the young man who was interpreting for me, "Ask them what they want prayer for." He would come back and describe their prayer request, which was often for a terrible headache, backache, or something of the sort.

But one of the greatest miracles happened when he was speaking to a young Haitian woman who walked up to me holding a baby. She looked so sad. I noticed my interpreter's countenance change while he was listening to her. He looked surprised, yet delighted. I said, "What does she want prayer for?" My interpreter said, "She wants to be a Christian!" The Heavens were open and we led her to the Lord!

After I prayed for a deaf man, I said to my interpreter, "Ask him if he can hear." The man told the interpreter, "A little bit."

I said, "Hallelujah, that's good, but not good enough. We serve the God of completion." I prayed a second time and said to my interpreter. "Ask him can he hear, now?"

My interpreter asked the gentleman and this time he said, "Better."

I said, "Hallelujah, that's good, but not good enough." I prayed a third time. This time when my interpreter asked the precious, Creole-speaking man if he could hear, the man looked me in the eyes and said, "Hallelujah!"

We serve the God of miracles.

Increased Grace

I am still amazed by the *grace* that the Lord kept me under. Upon returning to the U.S., I stayed up all night at the Houston airport, creating a slide show of mission trip photos while waiting for an early morning flight. I arrived in Phoenix the next morning, wrote a sermon, had the media team put the slide show on our conference laptop, and went directly into a meeting at 7:00 P.M.

To this day, since my return from Haiti, I have had an increased level of grace to be able to see the rubble, the devastation, and the pain, yet have the ability to rise above it and "go" not looking away. I have an increased level of love, compassion, healing, and impartation. I believe this is true because the anointing increases as we go for we are *commanded* to go. Divine Love is in "the field," and we can glean as much we chose, just like Ruth.

Following is a prophetic letter that I wrote Easter morning during our trip to Haiti.

Harvest in Haiti

To the Church:

There's a magnificent sunrise as I celebrate Easter morning in Haiti. As I write this, I am surrounded by the beauty of the Creator, yet surrounded by rubble. The devastation in this nation is almost incomprehensible to the human mind. John 12:24 says, *"Unless a seed is planted in the soil and dies, it remains alone. But its death will produce many new seeds—a plentiful harvest of new lives"* (NLT). Many, many seeds have fallen to the earth in Haiti, and it is time for a plentiful harvest here. We have ministered to 1.1 million people in three days! I plead with the Church of Jesus Christ to remember the precious Haitians. No human being should have to live like this. Miles and miles of tent cities...all beds of rock.

To the Haitian People:

The Lord would say to Haiti: "I love you; I love you; I love you. I have heard the wailing. I have seen the tears. I have your tears in a bottle. I am about to show Myself mighty and bring joy to your nation. I am going to use Haiti to extend new mercies of God each morning and to remind My people that Jesus came to serve, not to be served."

The Lord says: "Haiti is going to be an example of how church and government will work side by side. For it was never His intention that church and state be separated. It is God who places those in authority whom He chooses and ordains for this hour, for this day, for this time. The government rests on His shoulders and the earth is His and the fullness thereof."

The Lord would say to Haiti: "I am bringing trucks and bulldozers, trucks and bulldozers, trucks and bulldozers. As in the days of Nehemiah when the walls were rebuilt, the enemy will laugh and say it cannot be done, that you cannot revive the stones from the dusty rubble, that even a fox could knock down your walls. But I have come to proclaim that rebuilding that was completed in history in 52 days can be completed very quickly again. For God is sending a wind of acceleration, acceleration, acceleration. You will feel the cool breeze of this wind of acceleration, and it will literally lower the temperatures in your nation."

"It is I, it is I, it is I," says the Lord, "who *builds the house, so they labor not in vain*. Haiti will be a shining example of Isaiah 60:10, for the foreigners will come and rebuild the land, and kings will minister. The Lord became poor so Haiti can be rich."

CHAPTER **10**

A NEW PATH

By Bione D. Riggio

Unemployed, but serving the Lord full-time in Las Vegas, Nevada

At one time I had a multi-million dollar construction company. We went bankrupt in October of 2009. I had always given mightily, not only personally, but out of my business with tithes, offerings, alms, and so forth. I was pretty disappointed at first. But God showed up in my life like never before. When I was at my weakest, He was at His strongest. I have received many words and prophecies since then. When my company was doing well, I was very comfortable. When this came about, I had a few decisions to make about what to do with my life, but I decided to *press in* to God.

I believe my construction business was always Plan B. I have become more patient while waiting on the Lord. I have never had much idle time in my life. When I was going through bankruptcy, I had a number (dollar wise) that I thought I would be left with. Only God gave me three times that much. I also felt like I needed to get outside my church. I believe God is about to bless my family and me with new businesses and finances. I believe that answering the call to go to Haiti, and all I learned there, will be an important part of all I do in the future.

Learning to Pray for Others

Before going to Haiti, I didn't pray for people much even though our church encourages praying for others all the time. I felt that if God didn't heal them, it was my fault and that they could get a better leader to pray for them. But one night in Haiti, Curtis prayed for and released spiritual gifts into the team. The gifts that God gave to me through Curtis ignited a fire in me to pray for the Haitian people. I couldn't wait to pray for people. I could have stayed at the crusade all night, and I was probably the last team member in the crowd at the end of each night. I was blessed to hang around people like Kelley Murrell and Richard Barton and watch them pray for people per Joan's teaching. It was awesome, not a drawn-out process at all. I was really impressed by the simplicity of it all, and I learned so much.

I was blessed to be able to go on this trip to Haiti! It was *unbelievable* how smoothly everything went and how anointed the trip was. I was honored to be around all these mighty men and women of God. I am thankful for the many friends that I made in Haiti. They all poured into my life encouragement and even prophetic insight. What a blessing! We saw divine appointment after divine appointment, and I just knew it was God. I have been blessed to go and am looking for more blessings, favor, grace, mercy, revelation, and discernment from being associated with Joan Hunter Ministries.

Pressing in More

I returned home from Haiti feeling very pumped up by the Holy Spirit and what happened through the team. I have been testifying to all types of people of what happened in Haiti. I belong to a big church, and quite a few people knew I was going and were praying for me. All the testimonies, pictures, and videos are being passed around, and thousands of people are hearing and seeing how good God is. Everyone I talk to was excited by the size of the crowds and the number of healings. I also find myself praying for people at church much more than I did in the past, especially when I see people in pain.

I really thought, before I left for this mission to Haiti, that I was pressing in to God like never before. Now I see that I need to push harder. What an *amazing* feeling it is to pray for someone and ask, "How do you feel?" and hear him or her respond, "I don't have any pain." It doesn't get much better than that.

CHAPTER 11

ANOINTING WARRIORS

By Mary Alves

Housewife/Almond Grower from Newman, California

Ever since I was born again in 2001, I have had a desire to go to the mission field. I went to New Orleans in 2007 with Operation Blessing, and it was an incredible experience. When I first heard about the trip to Haiti, I thought I would love to go. I began to pray about the trip, and when Joan came to my church and spoke about the Haiti trip at the meetings, I prayed, "Father, do You want me to go? I will go if You want me go." When I mentioned to some members of Joan Hunter Ministries that I was considering going on the trip, they counseled me to go. That was enough for me. Thankfully, as far as the funds to go, I was blessed to have the money in our savings. God supplies our every need.

I am grateful to the Lord who directed me to go on a mission to Haiti. He has done such an incredible work in me. Before that, I was in bondage to a spirit of fear for five years, but finally found deliverance in March of 2009. When we have a spirit of fear, our spiritual gifts will go dormant, and what we fear, we will honor more than God. We cannot have two masters. Now that the fear is gone, I can use the gifts God gave me. As I sought to move forward in my gifts, God directed me to Joan Hunter to receive training in the gifts of healing.

Passing It On

During our time in Haiti, God gave me a great love and compassion for people—I was truly changed through this experience. My hatred for oppression has also risen. Jesus came to set the captives free, and He has set me free. At times it was painful to see the poverty in Haiti. However, I was there sent by the Lord to be a servant for *Him* by praying with the Haitians for many needs.

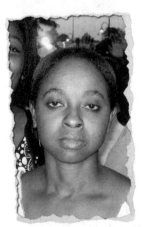

One of the greatest blessings was being able to be used by God to help set others free from the same spirit of fear that had plagued my life. There was a great anointing from the Lord for healing.

Many people came up to me full of fear. When I prayed it was like a light switch being turned on. Their eyes would become instantly brighter. They would raise their arms to the heavens, thanking Jesus for their healing, and then they would hug me.

One of the most touching moments for me occurred during the Easter service. Four people surrounded me asking for prayer at the same time. I placed them in a line, and when I was done praying for the first person, I looked up and saw that there were ten people waiting. Awesome! About 15 feet away, a tall, muscular man stood, looking at me with an expression of unbelief. I thought to myself, *Is he a security guard?* I knew that he was not.

As I prayed for the people in line, they would raise their arms in thanksgiving to the Lord. Each one would do this. I then noticed that this man was taking steps closer toward me until finally he was standing right next to me. He looked at me and said "I need prayer" (he spoke English).

I replied, "What is your need?"

He said, "I have asthma."

I replied, "Do you know Jesus?" (I always ask this question to people; it's most important.)

He said, "No, but I want to."

I began to prophesy for the first time, "You are a warrior for the Lord." As I pointed to the crowd, I told him, "God wants to set your people free, and He wants to work through you. When you accept Jesus as your Savior, please do not walk away like some do. Stay faithful to Him. He wants to work through you. If you stay obedient to the Lord, then your cup will overflow with great joy and you will not contain it."

I then asked him if he was married and had children. He said yes. I began to tell him that he would minister to his wife and children and that they would never be the same. Then I went on to ask him if he was ready to receive Jesus. He said yes and asked if he could get down on his knees. The warrior received Jesus, and then the Lord healed him from asthma. Then I led the warrior in a prayer for a mentor for him, a pastor, and a church. As I watched the warrior walk away, the overwhelming power of the Holy Spirit came over me.

Then all these little Haitian children surrounded me at once like angels. I placed my hands over their heads, praying for salvation and protection for them. I had to keep myself from crying because I had more praying to do. I thanked the Lord for this moment and for sending me to Haiti. What a blessing!

New Beginnings

When I returned from Haiti, I felt a sense of sadness because the impact of the experience was so great. On our journey, we ministered to the Haitians, witnessed God's healing power, and fell in love with the people of Haiti.

After the trip to Haiti the Lord led me to many new beginnings. I returned to my home in Newman, California, on Wednesday, April 7, and on Saturday, April 10, I began to participate in a ministry at my church, Calvary Temple in Modesto, for the first time. With this ministry, Nineveh Outreach, we set up at the parks and minister to the people in need. The Word is preached, people are born again, and we give out food and clothing to the needy. I pray for those who have a physical, spiritual, or emotional need just like in Haiti. I see that America is not so different from Haiti. Many need Jesus!

One of the pastors asked me to be a leader of the prayer team and also asked me to preach the Gospel. On May 1, we had a Women's Conference at Calvary Temple. I was asked to be an altar worker (minister to women) for the first time, and the Lord healed many of the women at the conference. The anointing was very powerful. After the experience I gained in Haiti, the Lord has given me greater boldness to lay hands on the sick and minister deliverance to people—and He has given me an overall greater love for others.

A couple of days after my return, my husband, Daniel, and I also found out that we were receiving a tax refund that was not expected. This covered the expense of my trip. Thank You, Jesus! He truly has been faithful to me from beginning to end!

CHAPTER 12

DIVINE SET-UP

By Glenda Abbe

High School Substitute Teacher from Raleigh,
North Carolina

God is an awesome God. I had blocked March 30th through April 6th for a mission trip to Cuba, but that trip was postponed to the fall. God had another plan for me during this week. I have been doing short-term mission trips for 18 years, and nothing makes me happier than serving Him on the mission field. When the Cuban trip changed, I immediately began looking for a way to serve in Haiti during this week. When I received the e-mail on February 4th about the Healing4Haiti trip, I immediately answered the call. I thought it was pretty significant that the days were exactly the days I had set aside for the other trip. Before I knew I would be able to go, I packed my bedroll, just in case I would need it to sleep on the floor.

I am a retiree and depend totally on offerings to be able to go on all my mission trips. God has never let me down. He knows the desire of my heart is to serve Him on the mission field. I quickly sent out a few letters, and more than half of what I needed came in right away. I had no doubt that all would be provided before I left, and it was!

Faith in the Rubble

It was sad to see the devastation left by the earthquake in Haiti and to know that hundreds or maybe even thousands were still missing and buried under some of the rubble we saw. Even being there and hearing their personal stories, it was hard to imagine what they really went through and how they felt. The poverty of the people is overwhelming. Many of the little boys had no clothes from the waist down and some children wore just underwear or tattered clothes. Most of us left our clothes and shoes and other supplies we brought. It was amazing, though, to see how God was using this terrible tragedy to turn this nation toward Him. Although we did have the opportunity to lead souls to Jesus, we actually met more Christians than non-Christians. In the hospital we visited, everyone we talked to was a Christian.

At the pastor's conference, Joan had them hold up their pocketbooks as she prayed a prayer over their finances. Joan would have normally taken an offering, giving them the opportunity to give a seed offering. But she knew they were without jobs and had little resources so she did not take an offering. We were all surprised and humbled as they all came running to the platform to leave an offering. It was amazing to hear the testimony of some who got jobs the next day.

At the healing services, it was such a blessing seeing the smiles on people's faces as they were healed. There were blind eyes that saw, deaf ears that heard, mutes that spoke, lame ones who didn't need their crutches, and many who left without pain, but there's no greater joy than the joy of seeing them born again. There were over one million people at the healing services. Joan prayed a prayer over all of them for God to heal their hearts of the trauma they experienced. It's a medical fact that trauma like this can cause other sicknesses in the body later, like cancer.

We praise God for the healing of their trauma and for the future sicknesses prevented by the healing of all those people who attended these services. I praise God for giving me the desire of my heart—to minister in Haiti. Thank You, Jesus.

God's Faithfulness

The day before I was to leave on this trip, I got word from my CPA that I would owe $20,000 in income taxes because of a bad financial deal. There was no way I could pay that. I refused to let the enemy steal my victory before I left on my trip, and I left this situation at the altar. After returning, I found out that I only owed $1,842—which I could handle—and I give God the glory.

This is a trip I will never forget. My church was blessed to see my photos and to hear the testimonies. I have been invited to join another ministry team in July, so I plan to return then. I love working for Jesus and doing my part in fulfilling the Great Commission.

Then Jesus came to them and said, "All authority in heaven and on earth has been given to Me. Therefore go and make disciples of all nations, baptizing them in the name of the Father and of the Son and of the Holy Spirit, and teaching them to obey everything I have commanded you. And surely I am with you always, to the very end of the age" (Matthew 28:18-20 NIV).

CHAPTER 13

BEAUTY FOR ASHES

BY LAURA BAKER

Employee of Joan Hunter Ministries from Pasedena, Texas

I happened to be working on site at Joan Hunter Ministries in the afternoon of the day that Joan received the invitation to Haiti. When she told me about it, my mouth dropped open and the first words out of my mouth were, "I want to go!" In my mind, I thought, *How can you go? You are the newest employee and only work part-time for the ministry. You will probably need to help answer phones at the office while others go.* But from that point on, I had a strong stirring inside of me that I could not shake.

Finally, at some point in February, I was bold enough to ask Joan if she wanted me to go to Haiti or to help in the office with phones. I had put off asking. I didn't want to hear the words "You need to stay here." Her answer was not what I expected, but rather "It's not what do *I* want you to do; it's what does *God* want you to do?" I was pretty sure I knew the answer to that one! Then, I *really* got excited!

I had no idea how I would pay for my trip, but I was never worried or even concerned about the money. I am not sure I even thought about the money part of it at that point. That had to be God because, in the natural, my finances didn't look very good. However, God provided and made a way for me to go to Haiti. A friend of mine called me on the day of the Super Bowl and told me God had told her to give me $500. When she called me, she told me she didn't know why God told her to give me that amount, but she was sure I would know what it was for. Immediately, I heard the Holy Spirit say *"Haiti."* Believe me, there were any number of other areas of my personal finances that the $500 could have gone to, but I never even had a thought of using it for anything but the trip to Haiti. The $500 paid the majority of the cost of the airfare to Haiti, and I had just enough "extra" in my account to cover the rest.

Knowing I had God's OK to go, I started getting the immunizations. Much to my surprise, my insurance covered most of the cost, so I paid very little compared to the actual cost. I still needed to come up with $600 for lodging, meals, and other accommodations. I thought I would sell some gold jewelry to get that money, but then I got another phone call that God had taken care of the $600 for me. *Praise God!* About four days before the trip, I felt led to sell some of my jewelry and was able to get enough money to buy many items needed in Haiti. I had just enough left over to make a cash donation in the amount I felt God had put in my heart to give. Truly, in preparing for this trip, God showed me how He gives provision for the things He calls us to do.

Sorrow in the Streets

When we arrived, I saw the truth of what I had heard. Haiti had been utterly devastated. People were so traumatized they could barely lift their heads. Hundreds of orphans have a safe place to play and one meal a day, but no bed or home to call their own. Many orphans have no shoes, some lack pants or shorts, and some do not even have underwear. New mothers with no hope for the future and no joy in their eyes lay next to their newborn babies and malnourished children. Young and old looked deep into our eyes for something to take their pain away. The emotional trauma was so great that many children and adults couldn't sleep because of nightmares and fear of another earthquake.

We saw block after block of rubble mixed with personal items like ruined clothes and broken dishes. It seemed like we were just circling the same block, but we were not. Row after row, block after block, field after field of makeshift tents served as homes for those whose homes no longer existed. Young and old alike were bathing in small ditches and in water used for anything and everything. A little boy at an orphanage, maybe eight years old, kept coming to me. He looked deep into my eyes, never with a smile, only sadness, and repeated his name, and my name, over and over and over. I never will forget him.

Sorrow Turned to Joy

There were 700 pastors and leaders at the pastors' training conference. They lacked joy and enthusiasm in the beginning. They were almost skeptical, and they were full of trauma. But I also saw many of those same pastors get free of trauma and hopelessness. They left smiling and healed. They had prayed for themselves and for others and watched God release His healing. They had been empowered to hope again and to embrace joy, even in the midst of suffering.

One night, many of the pastors determined to press to the front of the meeting to give an offering, even though it had been announced that there would be no offering received. Through their extravagant and generous hearts, the spirit of poverty was broken from their lives. This too released new levels of hope and joy as they looked to the future believing that God would bless and provide.

At the evening healing services, thousands of people received Christ as their Lord and Savior through a massive group prayer of salvation. Thousands of people were also freed of trauma, fear, grief, and headaches by laying hands on their hearts and heads and praying a massive "group" prayer. During the one-on-one minis-try time, many of the people whom I met had their heads down and just pointed to the area of their body that needed healing. After I prayed for them, they would look up and smile, make eye contact, and say, "Merci, Jesus" (Thank You, Jesus) because they had been healed and set free from trauma and pain. Children four to eight years old often took our hands and pulled us to someone they knew needed prayer. Their hope and faith were contagious, and many received healing from God. Truly, the manifestation of

God's peace and joy came upon thousands, replacing the trauma, fear, grief, and physical and emotional pain.

Not only were people being healed, but praise and worship increased to new levels with each night. As people encountered God's love and healing power, their joy and their worship of Him magnified. The most amazing time happened at the end of the Easter Sunday evening service. They didn't want to leave, and neither did we. Everything was shaking, but it wasn't an earthquake this time. People were praising God and rejoicing in what He had done. We all witnessed that God loves His people in Haiti, and as they cry out to Him in desperation, He hears them and answers them!

Focus on What *He's* Doing

It was a privilege and an honor to be a part of the mission. One of the main things I learned relates to my focus. When we returned, I was comparing the water pressure to what we had in Haiti. The Holy Spirit convicted me and said, "Don't focus on the negative." It was a great reminder to me that no matter what the inconveniences were and how great the devastation we witnessed was, my focus must stay on the mighty work that God is doing in Haiti and His goodness to us while we were there.

God gave me two Scriptures while we were in Haiti on Good Friday morning. Isaiah 54:10 says, *"'Though the mountains be shaken and the hills be removed, yet My unfailing love for you will not be shaken nor My covenant of peace be removed,' says the Lord who has compassion on you"* (NIV). And in Matthew 11:4-5, Jesus said, *"Go back and report to John what you hear and see: the blind receive sight, the lame walk, those who have leprosy are cured, the deaf hear, the dead are raised, and the good news is preached to the poor"* (NIV).

Since the trip to Haiti, God has given me more courage and boldness to pray for people in places I might not have before. I am willing to pray for anyone, anywhere—without worrying about what he or she would think or what the outcome is. Before the trip to Haiti, I knew God *could* use me, not because I am special at all, but because His Word says so, because I yield myself to His plans, and because He can do whatever He wants to do! But in Haiti, He showed me how much He *would* use me and others when we just set ourselves aside for *His purpose only,* obey Him, and follow His leading! I am very thankful to God for the privilege and opportunity to be a part of the Healing4Haiti team to touch His people in Haiti for His glory!

CHAPTER 14

PREACHING BEYOND MY REGION

BY JANIS PETERS

Associate Pastor at MorningStar Ministries in Rossville, Illinois, and Owner of Janis Peters & Associates, a registry of caregivers to assist families in finding solutions to their loved ones' needs

The Lord certainly orchestrated the details of this trip. It was truly a faith walk experience. I had been seeking the Lord during February, telling Him, "I will do anything, Lord." I knew He was stirring me up to change my directions a bit. I was yielding myself, and then one morning the Scripture came to "preach beyond my region" (see 2 Cor. 10:16).

Presently, I'm an associate pastor at MorningStar Ministries in Rossville, Illinois. I have also been involved in marketplace ministry primarily within the county, and I have a care-giving service that provides caregivers for the elderly. I have a very large registry of people who come to me for assistance in finding a job and also people who need caregivers. My territory is large.

Just before this Scripture came, I had stepped out of my county (region), so I was praising God that I really was preaching the Gospel beyond my region! But looking back now, I don't think that was what He had in mind.

What I Was Born For

Let me give you some personal history. In 1988, the Holy Spirit ministered to me in a powerful dream and showed me God's awesome power to heal. Then, in 1996, I had another dream in which the Lord was using His presence through my hands to release creative miracles. I saw a woman's fingers grow out as I patted her hands. The Holy Spirit said, "This is why you were born, Janis." The impact and power of God was so strong from those dreams, I believe I was "under the influence" for days!

At the time of the first dream, I was in a denominational church with no Spirit-filled influence, so the dream was not tracking with my religious teaching. When I shared my experience, people were not receptive, so I had to keep seeking.

I have been pursuing the call of God on my life to see these things happen. I have been laying hands on the sick; I have been reading and studying on how to heal the sick. My ministry of care-giving has opened doors for me to minister to those who are dying or in need of healing, to those suffering loss and emotional distress. I have seen the power of God in action daily. But I knew there was more.

After these dreams, I had a real-life experience in a nursing home. As I was praying and laying hands on five people in the room, I was very much aware of being in the Spirit. I reached across a bed to lay hands on a gentleman, and as I did, I felt like I was in a third world country. The man had all his fingers and part of his feet amputated; the smell was awful and he was so thin and wasted. I kept praying, but there was more happening in me. I didn't see his healing, but I knew God was reminding me that He was going to show off soon.

I had been reading a journal by a surgeon in Chicago, Illinois. He had spent a week in Haiti and had sent messages on his blackberry journaling his days. I was enthralled. I told the Lord, "Oh, I can't medically help those people, but I am so full of Your Spirit; surely there is a place for me."

One morning I remembered the postcard Joan Hunter had sent out. I checked my passport; it was active, but ready to expire the next month. I told my husband that I was being led to go to Haiti. "Just make sure it is God," he said so sweetly.

I called Eric Cummings, but he said that only 34 could come. The trip was full. After a day of calls and wondering, however, I received the OK to join the trip at about 8 P.M. My blackberry beeped just as I finished teaching a Wednesday evening group. I looked up at everyone and said, "I am going to Haiti with Joan Hunter Ministries!" Shortly after that, a dear friend called and said, "You are going. Let's get your flights secured." She paid for the entire cost of my flight. This was the 4th of March. I was already behind. But God has blessed me with people who love me and who have stood by me. Offerings were taken for my trip and people sent me money. Substantial contributions were made by a hospital and a doctor who had previously been in Haiti. I e-mailed for help financially, I went for shots, and I was given an offering for the $600.00 on the Sunday after it had to be in. The Lord made a way, and before I knew it, the time to leave had arrived.

And It Began

The only way for me to give credibility to the following pages is to tell you that I saw, I touched, I heard, and I loved, just as in First John 1:1.

On March 30, 2010, I got on the plane to Port-au-Prince with 35 other people whom I had just met. Immediately, we were in unity of purpose and our hearts were ready for the adventure ahead. Our *fearless* leader Eric yelled out, "Game on!" and we set out to do the job God had called us to do. It was amazing the bonding that took place that day. After arriving at the beautiful mission house, we got to know each other and had a time of fellowship after our evening meal. We heard each person tell how God brought him or her to Haiti. It was wonderful to experience the love that flowed that evening.

As we traveled every day in a yellow school bus, we saw crumbled buildings, countless people setting up shop along the roads, and almost everyone selling the same things. Every day, in the unbearably hot sun they were sitting and waiting for someone to buy something from them.

Our first meeting was powerful. Over 700 ministers and church leaders listened as Joan Hunter taught on healing and financial prosperity. The Spirit of the Lord settled in on the conference as they were taught how to heal the sick. At first there was a hesitancy to believe, but when the healings happened, they received it eagerly.

After the first day, we were allowed to minister to individuals. We made ourselves available out in the grassy area of the compound. One by one the ministers and lay leaders allowed us to lay hands on them and pray for specific needs. The love on their faces and expressions of God's Holy Spirit were priceless. I prayed for some precious women and a couple of men. I even received requests to pray that several would be blessed with children! What an awesome request in such a land.

One special moment I witnessed was a supernatural offering. Joan was talking about how an offering is taken, but said that here in Haiti she was not going to do that because of the deep poverty and present level of joblessness. Instead, while she was talking someone threw some money on the table, and it was like a call to arms! The whole place exploded into motion and people were bringing what they had and putting it on the table. A hat was filled and another container brought. It was so moving to be a part of such expectation! I heard that one man received an offer for employment with the government the day after and was giving praise.

After the final session of teaching, Joan had all the people in attendance line up outside the tent side by side so she could lay hands on them to receive the anointing. All the team members received that touch too! Glory to God!

Declaration of Hope

The three-day crusade in the heart of Port-au-Prince was like a dream come true. I had a poster on my wall at home of a crusade that showed a million people in attendance. My heart cried out to see such a crusade and be a part of it. The Bible says that He will give us the desires of our heart (see Ps. 37:4), and He did! It was estimated that 1.1 million people came from all over Haiti to experience this Resurrection weekend, and I saw them! There were people on the street waiting to have someone touch them. I saw them. I heard them sing, and I watched them dance. In the midst of crumbled ruins and the smell of death, hope was offered and a declaration was made. *"Healing is coming to Haiti! Put your hand on your heart and say this prayer!"* Then Joan prayed to release the people from the spirit of trauma, and an awesome release from pain and fear occurred throughout the crowd.

Personally, I cannot tell how many people I prayed for. At one point, I stretched out my hand and just walked along the barricade and touched any who would reach out and touch me, praying all the while that the anointing that breaks yokes and relieves burdens would be released into those dear people. People were saved, delivered, filled with the Spirit, and healed! My interpreters were blessed. I asked my first one if he had received the Holy Spirit and he said, "No but I want to now." It was wonderful to pray for him and see his spirit receive what God had for him. While we were singing and praising at the beginning of the next service, he turned to me and said, "I can heal the sick now because I am filled with the Holy Spirit!" He was just glowing.

Another man came to me and said he would interpret for me. He was a uniformed guard for us and very much impressed with what was happening. As he repeated over and over the prayers for salvation, infilling, deliverance, and healing, he couldn't handle it anymore. He was a tall, young man whom you would not want to tangle with if there was a problem. He said there was too much noise, so we went back to the shelter around the platform. I asked him if he was saved and he laughingly said, "I am Catholic!" So I told him that was fine, that God heard his prayers and answered them. He said it was hard to be good and live right when you were a cop.

Then he described what it had been like in the earthquake. I didn't know what to do! At that point he was giving me his heart's cry. He allowed me to pray and cast out the spirit of trauma and fear, and he was healed. Eric was with me too, and another uniformed guard came to him and presented himself for prayer, and he also was healed. When the last song was sung and high praise was being released, I saw one of the guards dancing his heart out on the platform. Glory to God!

Hospitals and Orphanages

Our days were planned and full; there were no idle moments. During the week we visited a hospital. I only saw a couple of doctors. The rooms were wards, and family members were helping. We prayed in the women's surgical recovery room where there were a large number of people. A young man came to me and wanted prayer. He was upset, but received peace from God. I went over to a lady in an upper body cast in a bed, and I put my hands on her shoulder above her cast and prayed. She yelled out in pain, and it startled me. I removed my hand and told the pain to leave and went on to pray for others. I then sat down outside to collect my thoughts on what I was witnessing. As I sat there, out walked the lady in the upper body cast. I just sat there watching her take her kids by the hand, smiling and walking. It was amazing!

At the orphanage of Pastor Rene Joseph, I struggled to get a grasp on what I was seeing. It was so dry and barren there, and all the children were assembling to see us and receive some food. The ladies of the community were cooking on open fires. The fires were made of sticks gathered like at a campout. Some big stainless pans were used to cook corn mush. It was primitive, and not one child received a drink while we were there. Water is not readily available, and the need to dig wells is pressing.

The children stared at us in wonder as well. We must have been a sight with our cameras, water bottles, backpacks, sunglasses, and hats. They had some clothes, but one little guy had a t-shirt on and that was all! The children who had sponsors wore uniforms for school. These children have lost parents and family members in the quake. They are living in homes that have opened to them and may receive one meal a day and a banana. One little boy, maybe six years of age, latched onto me. He went everywhere with me and would not let go. I believe the Lord was talking to me the whole time, and the boy was receiving a sweet peace that he doesn't have very often. God bless Pastor Rene for his vision and passion to help the orphans of Haiti.

The next orphanage we went to was full of babies. There were enough for each team member to hold and love. Their situation was a little different because their families were intact, but couldn't care for their needs. Our hearts cried out over the great need for the orphans in Haiti.

Breakthroughs at Home

I have been broadened and stretched as I fell in love with the Haitian people. When God says, "Go," we must not hesitate. He wants to bless us and use us to propel His Gospel to people who are hungry and thirsty for Him.

I realize more than ever that the Holy Spirit is speaking to us to walk in faith. Reliving the trip to Haiti is full of all kinds of emotions, and I have been experiencing them all. There is a song that says "Take me out of my mind into Your Spirit...." That is where I have been. It was an adventure I will never forget.

On the flight home, I was able to minister to two women who were cousins. I sat next to the window, and the lady in the aisle side seat had a broken leg. Her cousin in the center seat began to tell me all about her allergies and her life. I could feel a set-up coming on so I just listened to the Lord and waited for my open door. Then the unthinkable happened; the lady with the broken leg got up and switched places with her cousin!

She began talking, and I asked if I could pray for her healing, telling her of my trip to Haiti. She agreed, but added something else, "I have MS." I told her the Lord could take care of that too! So I prayed the prayers for healing, and she received. She turned to her cousin and told her to let me pray for her, and she did. Both were so touched and full of His presence they didn't know what to do. I began to teach them some concepts they needed, and before we knew it, the plane was landing in Indy. Those two women got off the plane brand-new and refreshed!

On the first Sunday morning back, as the closing prayer was given at church, a woman and her daughter came through the doors and walked to the front for prayer. That lady was in her late 50s and physically a mess. I had been ministering to her since the fall, but she couldn't see what God wanted to give her. The doctor had told her she was dying and there was no hope. But she had left the hospital against his wishes. There she was with her cane and bruises where she was bleeding internally. She wanted me to pray for her. She grabbed me and held me tightly.

We stood there for a long time in front of the congregation just hugging, and I whispered in her ear that God loved her. I prayed in the Spirit, while others sat in awe and prayed with us; it was amazing. Her daughter was in tears and visibly moved by the experience. I told the lady that Jesus had healed her. What did she want? She told me she wanted to know her sins were forgiven, in case she did die, so that she would know where she was going! That morning she was born again and became a new creation. A week later she walked into church a new woman. She is still under a doctor's care, but stronger than ever and full of life. Praise the Lord!

My daughter Sally gave birth by C-section to a wonderful baby boy in the middle of April. The surgery was planned because of some difficulty, and the baby lost a lot of blood and was in need of a transfusion. I remembered what Joan had taught about praying for people who have had transfusions. There is a definite connection between people when blood is received from another person. It is a spiritual concept of the bloodline, so I prayed for my little grandson after the transfusion took place. The doctors and nurses couldn't get over how quickly he responded and how peaceful he became. Thank You, Jesus.

No Weapon

After returning home I also saw an incredible financial provision! I am praising God for His supernatural provision. I had to receive shots in order to go to Haiti, and my time was short to get it done. In the process, there was a battery of blood work that was done without cause. The cost was beyond me. I received a bill for over $2,600 a couple days before the trip. I almost fainted, but decided to keep on trusting God.

After returning, before church one Sunday, the Lord told me to give an extra $35 as seed money to take care of this bill. I did that and planned to visit the CEO of the hospital. He was aware of the problem and had told me to give the bill to him. The Lord told me when to go. I asked Him to send angels for help and to orchestrate His perfect timing for me to speak with this gentleman. When I arrived, he was not there so the secretary took the bills to copy and make an appointment. But God had the CEO walk in just then, and we were able to chat. After explanations were given, I asked him if I could tell him what I had done in Haiti. The Lord spoke through me, and it was anointed. The CEO told me not to worry about the bill and that it would be taken care of! He said that even if he had to pay it himself, it would be taken care of. I walked out in awe and full of praise for the blessing of the Lord.

CHAPTER 15

BLESSED BY DADDY GOD

BY RICHARD BARTON

*Part Owner and Director of Operations of Global Vending
and Co-founder of Lead by Faith 4 Him from
Columbus, Texas*

I have felt a call on my life to go to the mission field, but was waiting on God's timing. My daughter graduates in three years, and I thought I would enter the field then.

Then, at a meeting at 4 Corners, Joan Hunter's church, I heard Joan announce that she had been invited to take a team to Haiti. I felt a stirring in my spirit and took her advice to pray about going. A week later, I felt I was to go, but I was worried about finances and the cost of the trip. I owed $3,400 in back taxes. I prayed and told God that I would go if He provided the money. My wife didn't mind my going, but she didn't want to go. The next day I had a check on my desk for $4,000, more than enough to cover the taxes. I knew this was my answer from God.

I told Joan at the next meeting that I was to go on the trip and had my wife's blessing. I got as much info on Haiti as I could, and the Holy Spirit started nudging my wife. She got more and more interested and asked if she could go. We prayed about it and came into agreement, and she was accepted to go. I was thrilled. Then the money started coming in for passports, immunizations, plane tickets, living cost in Haiti, and all the supplies we needed. Our faith never dwindled, and all of our needs were met right on time—praise Jesus. We knew this trip was of God because all the finances came in and our company wasn't going to charge us vacation time for going.

However, the Holy Spirit wasn't finished. He kept doing a mighty work on my wife. She attended a couple of services where Joan preached, and she started going to church with me at 4 Corners. Her faith came alive. The Holy Spirit put it in her heart to be ordained through Joan Hunter Ministries, and I was thrilled. We made 4 Corners our home church, and we tithe faithfully, and God is still pouring out His blessings on us. We started our own ministry and teamed up with another ministry. I always believed I would have a ministry, but now my wife has become involved with it and is so on fire for God. That has been my biggest reward from Daddy God—to have my wife sharing my dreams and vision and to get us one step closer to full-time ministry. We are most thankful to Joan Hunter and her ministry for her vision and her apostolic covering. I am a proud member of the 4 Corners Alliance, and I feel blessed as a result. And all these miracles happened even before we stepped foot in Haiti!

Grown-Out Legs and Happy Children

We experienced so much during our time in Haiti; it would be impossible to convey it all to you. We saw so much need and so much victory.

For example, on the third day of our trip, we visited a hospital. The roof was held up with jacks and braces. There was no electricity, no lights, and no A/C. It was dismal and gloomy. My group was assigned to visit the surgery ward, and it was worse than words can describe. We prayed for everyone, and one man's leg grew out. He was healed and went home. Others got saved and were freed from the spirit of trauma and fear. One man asked if we came all the way from America for their sake. We said yes. It changed my life as I saw the Holy Spirit flow through us like I have never seen before.

Toward the end of the trip, we journeyed out and saw Pastor Rene Joseph's new orphanage. The team was able to play and interact with 300-400 orphans. We also had the opportunity to feed them. The kids were blessed with toys and balls we brought with us. They blessed us because, even in the poorest of living conditions, they were happy. The next day, we went to another orphanage for kids from newborn to 4 years old. Everyone had a blast holding and loving on the infants and toddlers. Yes, even the men turned to Jell-O® over those kids because they were so happy and all they wanted was to be loved. We had a hard time leaving.

One Million Reaching for God

I saved the best for last. The crusades consisted of three big evening meetings that totaled over one million people in attendance. The Haitians were coming out for a touch from God. The whole team got a chance to lay hands on people. We couldn't pray fast or long enough because the people were so hungry for a touch of God. The Holy Spirit showed up in a big way and everyone got healed.

I saw a blind man get new eyes and a girl with a crushed arm receive total healing. A baby who had shown no vital signs for several days was brought back to life. Many people were healed of styes and digestive issues due to the unsanitary conditions. Backs and legs were healed. People were delivered from headaches, mumps, blindness, and muteness. The list goes on and on.

I thought my faith was high after getting my own vision back years ago, but seeing the Holy Spirit working through the team caused my faith to skyrocket. Many people were freed from demonic forces and gave their hearts to Jesus. I lost count.

When Easter came, we went to a celebration at the crusade site with several local churches and joined in lots of praise and worship; it was an awesome time.

Forever Changed

Through this trip, the Lord confirmed my dream for the mission field; my faith grew on this trip, and my life feels complete. Best of all, my wife now shares the same dream and vision. The most exciting part is seeing her on fire for God and growing in her faith. I can't wait to see what God has in store for us next.

Truly, my life will be forever changed. I saw all of Heaven walk with us, and the Holy Spirit flowed in miracles, signs, and wonders. I saw a broken people who had more faith and belief in Jesus than I could have imagined. It was the trip of a lifetime.

I have attended a couple healing services since coming home and the healings are still going on strong. My corporate sponsors have even had their eyes opened, and after seeing the pictures and videos of the mission trip, they also have had a change of heart toward spiritual healing. This has also been an awesome opportunity to talk about God and share the Gospel.

God has blessed us and blessed us. While we were on the trip, we were told that we would probably not have jobs when we returned. However, we believed that if this door closed, God would open another. When we got back, not only did we still have our jobs, but I got a raise. We are moving to bigger and better office space, and we have had an influx of capital to purchase new equipment.

Recently I had to run to Wal-Mart for some items for my job. I asked for help, and a transvestite clerk gave me assistance. I thought, *This is the ugliest transvestite I have ever seen,* and I didn't say anything to him because I was in a hurry and my crews were waiting on me.

He helped me find my items, and I headed for the checkout, but I noticed that he was following me. He finally asked what the symbols were on my shirt (it has five symbols that describe the Good News). I explained the symbols and shared the Gospel with him. He asked me if Jesus could love someone like him. I walked him through dealing with unforgiveness, trauma, and stress. We bound and cast out the spirit of homosexuality and all other hindering spirits. He then accepted Jesus into his heart and was saved. This took almost an hour.

He asked me to wait for him and I did, thanking the Father for using me. He came back out and his hair was wet because he had washed out his hairdo. The earrings and makeup were all gone. He introduced himself and thanked me for taking the time to lead him to Jesus.

This confused individual was now the man God had intended him to be. I almost missed it. I had been disgusted with his appearance and lifestyle instead of seeing the lost and hungry soul inside. I thank the Holy Spirit for opening my eyes and for my training at Joan Hunter Ministries. I was equipped and ready and didn't realize it.

Though the trip to Haiti is over, by no means is this the end. I believe it is only the beginning. Our ministry is moving forward, we are in prayer and preparation for upcoming trips, and we are learning more about the gifts of the Spirit. I am blessed and satisfied, but wanting more of God.

CHAPTER 16

OVERCOME

BY CATHERINE BARTON

*Office Manager of Global Vending and Co-founder of Lead
by Faith 4 Him from Columbus, Texas*

My husband, Richard, told me that Joan Hunter Ministries
had been invited to go to Haiti and that he felt he should go
with them. I wasn't at peace with the idea at all. According to the
media, there were still tremors! But we attended a miracle service
with Joan Hunter at 4 Corners Church one night, and Joan spoke
of the upcoming trip to Haiti. That night, a peace came over me,
and I knew that Richard was supposed to go. We were at work the
following week, and he asked me to watch a video about Haiti. At
that moment, I knew I was supposed to go too. The details would
work themselves out. Through the process, I also decided to go

through ordination training with Joan Hunter Ministries, and it was truly incredible.

Meanwhile, Richard sent out an e-mail to the companies and distributors that we do business with, asking for donations to help finance the trip. These are all secular companies, but the funds started coming in within days! Thank You, Jesus! We were able to pay for the entire trip.

We Have It Made

During the trip, I received a better appreciation for what I have. Everywhere we went, there was devastation. The country is covered with fallen buildings and rubble. There is no electricity, trash lines the streets, and most people have only one meal a day. Yet the people were generally happy and content with what they had. There were children without shoes, playing and flying kites. Some had very minimal clothing or none at all. Even at the orphanage, some of the children had no underwear or panties. Others had no shoes, or the shoes they had were too small, too big, or falling apart. But almost everyone had a ready smile. We as Americans don't realize it, but we have it made.

A Special Place

We returned to the States and my heart was so heavy. I wasn't ready to leave those amazing people. I wanted to let everyone know about Haiti, my experience, and the need that is still there. Anytime I try to talk about Haiti, I tear up or cry. Joan Hunter asked me and my husband to "tell them a little about Haiti" one night at a miracle service. When I was handed the microphone, I forgot all that I wanted to say. Talking about Haiti is difficult for me because it brings back memories of all the people, the food, the smells, and the team. There will always be a special place in my heart for Haiti, and I look forward to a return visit.

CHAPTER 17

A PERSONAL EARTHQUAKE

BY SHELIA "SUGAR" TRASK

Founder of Scarfree03Ministries of Healing and Restoration, Therapeutic Massage Therapist, and Nanny of a miracle baby from Galveston, Texas

I got to go to Haiti by praying and trusting God for the necessary finances, and He provided just that. Many donations and unexpected financial blessings came through. Even payments on my car were made in advance. Someone paid a bill for me, but things weren't going the way I thought they should go. I expected that once people knew I was going on a mission trip to Haiti, they would give, bless me, and send me on my way. However, many times I only got, "Well, that's nice," or "Be careful," or "You know it's not safe over there." Some went as far as making negative comments about the temperature and living conditions and then added, "I'll be praying." It was a bit discouraging.

Then, all of a sudden I received an e-mail from Joan Hunter Ministries saying, "We need the additional $600 by Friday at noon." That was only two days away. I contacted a few more people, but to no avail. Time was running out, and I was beginning to wonder if I would be able to go. Then I received another e-mail, only a few hours before the deadline, saying *paid in full!* Praise the Lord!

Culture Shock

When we arrived in Haiti, we were greeted at the airport by an awesome Congo band and then shuttled to the baggage area. We experienced a great deal of culture shock at baggage claim and immigration. We were maneuvered around like cattle. There were hundreds of people with baggage all over the floor and to us it looked like a chaotic mess, but to them it was business as usual. We had to keep our eyes on the others and our baggage while taking directions, and all this while the noise was deafening. It was exciting to me—all the people, all the new faces, and the new language. Finally all of the baggage was retrieved and we went to the mission on a school bus.

Our driver, Mono, drove at 50 miles per hour down these terrible roads filled with rocks, people, and other crazy drivers. Haitian drivers pass on either side of the road, blowing horns and talking French Creole. Everywhere we looked we saw tents for miles and miles. There were vendors on the streets everywhere and no stop signs or street lights. Haiti is a place to ride, not drive, because you need 36 pairs of eyes and great brakes to survive. This showed me that living in the States is a safe haven, despite having to put up with speed traps, lights, and signs.

The mission house was a paradise in the mountains, a beautiful home complete with cooks, but no television, radio, or phones. This was my kind of trip! We had all the necessities. There were times when we did not have water pressure, toilets to flush, or access to the Internet, but that was not our reason for being in Haiti. This place was a palace compared to the tent cities we saw driving in from the airport.

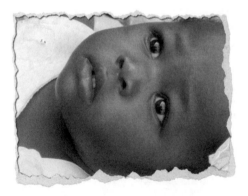

Haiti showed me how selfish I am and how I take God's love and blessings for granted. I repented and told the Lord how sorry I was for the way I had been wasting what He had given me. In a sense, I had my own personal earthquake. I realized that I needed Haiti as much as Haiti needed us as we ministered healing to these hungry people. It was refreshing in the natural as well as the spiritual.

The mission also changed how I view other ministries and organizations that ask Americans to help in relief for Africa, South America, Haiti, and so forth. The world is full of hurting people who need to be touched by God. It broke my heart to see those orphans crying out for more of Jesus. I now sponsor three Haitian orphans, and I have a burden for Haiti. I will be going back, sponsoring more children, and supporting the ministry.

CHAPTER 18

LORD, USE ME!

By Brian Guillory

Truck Driver from Tomball, Texas

God is blessing me financially and continues to do so in different ways every day. After I had decided to go on the trip, I contacted the church where I was first saved. I asked the pastor if he would pray about sponsoring me on my trip. He prayed about his part, and the next day he took up a love offering for me. Then my sister and I sent out a letter asking friends and family to sow into what God is doing in our lives. I think it is amazing to know that even non-Christian family members sowed into what God was doing. Praise God! God also moved on the heart of a dear friend to pay for my airplane ticket. Praise God for her obedience.

While I was in Kansas City, Missouri, getting my 18-wheeler repaired, a friend who owns a tax service invited me over to his house for dinner. It was a night of many miracles. We had a great dinner, and I got to pray for his daughter-in-law, who was having surgery the next day, and for his son, who was full of fear about the surgery. She came through the surgery perfectly and made a complete recovery. He also did my taxes and more than doubled my return. God's blessings are everywhere!

Finally, I went back to my original church, wondering if God was going to provide. And did He ever! After the service was over, I was talking to a few people who had asked about the trip. I was about to leave when a lady walked up to me and said that, after praying, she and her husband felt they were supposed to seed into my life and trip with a check for $1,000. Thank You, Jesus! With that, I was on my way to Haiti.

Hands and Feet

I must admit, I didn't know exactly what to expect in Haiti. It is hard to imagine something that you have never experienced. But I decided, no matter what we encountered, to allow God to use me in any way possible.

The house we stayed in was not damaged in the earthquake. That shows that God's hand of protection was upon all of us and Pastor Rene. The accommodations, the house staff, and the food were excellent. We were treated like royalty while we were there. I haven't tasted food so fresh and delicious in a long time. It was also a blessing to take a shower every day.

The weather was beautiful the whole trip. It might have been a little hot, but there was always a breeze at the house and when we were out ministering. I was told that it was supposed to be the beginning of the rainy season, but it only sprinkled a couple of times and that was refreshing.

Seeing the reaction of the pastors was exciting. Their hunger and enthusiasm during the two days of training was very encouraging. Looking at the faces of the individuals during the teaching sessions was nothing less than amazing. They were able to watch themselves and others being healed right in front of their eyes. It was easy to see that most had never seen someone healed. Thank You, God, for opening their eyes! May they take what they have learned, and may they be the hands and feet of Jesus.

The Healing Crusade was nothing short of miraculous. I personally prayed for over 200 people and saw many healings and miracles. I was sharing an interpreter with three other team members, and at one point he had walked over to help one of the ladies. A young woman walked up to me, but she couldn't understand English. I motioned with my hands to ask where she was experiencing pain. She motioned back, indicating that the pain was throughout her body. In times like this, it is extremely necessary to be sensitive to the Holy Spirit and to listen when He speaks.

I heard in my spirit *Fibromyalgia*. In the past, when I had prayed for people with this disease, they did not receive their healing. I had to choose whether to rely on past experiences or to *trust in God.* I trusted in God and prayed for her, and when I was done, she started slapping her body very hard and repetitively. My first thought was that she was manifesting unclean spirits, but I noticed that she was smiling and that all the pain was gone. We both started praising God with all that was in us. Watching her worship God with no pain in her body was a beautiful thing to behold.

The next miracle was just as exciting, if not better. A little old lady sitting in a wheelchair had been waiting patiently for several minutes. My interpreter came back to me and asked the lady what was wrong with her. We found out that she had fallen about a year ago and had injured her hip, legs, lower back, and knees. She had been in the wheelchair for a whole year. I prayed for new hips, knees, and lower back and for healing in her legs. I also cursed the spirit of trauma that was on her. My interpreter and I then helped her out of the wheelchair and she *walked!* She said that there was still a little pain so I prayed again, and then she said that all the pain was gone. She told my interpreter that she had not walked in over a year.

One of the things that touched me the most was visiting the orphanage and seeing the children. The children were so hungry to love, to play, and to be loved. Seeing the way the children help take care of their brothers and sisters, constantly looking after one another and making sure that they get enough to eat, really impacted me. Out of all the children, there was one little boy who blessed me the most. His name is Obierto. The excitement in his eyes, joy in his laughter, and warmth in his smile will stay with me forever. It was easy to see God's love in the face of this little boy.

One of my goals for the trip was to swim in the Caribbean Sea. It was a perfect end to a perfect trip. I hope to go back to Haiti on many other mission trips. My hope is that this experience will keep me from focusing on myself and will help me to reach out and touch the lives of men, women, and children—those who don't have enough or can't do for themselves—either by prayer, service, or giving. I want God to use me in all these ways.

Amazed by His Faithfulness

As we were getting ready to leave Haiti, I had mixed emotions. One part of me wanted to come back home and enjoy a warm shower, air conditioning, and my own bed. However, I also wanted to be in Haiti helping in any way possible. I was told before we left that part of my heart would be left in Haiti, and I know that it was a true statement.

After arriving back in the States, I found myself on a spiritual high that wouldn't stop. I felt so close to God that I thought I could not be attacked by the enemy, but I was wrong. I let down my guard for one minute and allowed the enemy to come in and get the better of me in one area. I thank the Lord for being my strength, my guide, and my comforter and for His forgiving, loving nature! Isaiah 40:29 says, *"He gives power to the weak, and to those who have no might He increases strength."*

I was determined to break off old mindsets, attitudes, and cycles that kept me in bondage and going around in circles most of my Christian life. I knew that I needed to focus on God and be patient. The Word of God says in Isaiah 40:31: *"But those who wait upon the Lord shall renew their strength; they shall mount up with wings like eagles, they shall run and not be weary, they shall walk and not faint."* The Word also says in Isaiah 54:10:

> *"The mountains shall depart and the hills be removed, but My kindness shall not depart from you, nor shall My covenant of peace be removed," says the Lord, who has mercy on you.*

Even though I knew I had been temporarily overcome, I also knew that the Lord has forgiven me, that He still has a purpose for me, and that I still could be used by God. God proved this by allowing me to minister to a co-worker and her husband. Watching God heal her husband was so reassuring that I girded myself in the armor of God and stood ready to be used and to fight the enemy if he dared to attack again.

Because I am ready to be used, I am going to be used. Since I got back from Haiti, God has used me to pray for several individuals, and they were healed of all manner of sickness and disease. God even gave me the opportunity to give my testimony about Haiti in front of a church. The Holy Spirit manifested His presence, and we had a healing service. I was also able to deliver several prophetic words and words of wisdom.

How great is God that He would use a man with no college education and no knowledge of public speaking, but a heart and willingness to serve and to be obedient? How great is God that He would choose to forgive and use a man who, before knowing Christ, committed sin after sin? I can say without doubt that I am forgiven and redeemed. With that I make one last confession. Lord, may I be obedient to go where I am sent and take You wherever I go.

CHAPTER 19

I LEFT MY HEART IN HAITI

BY MELISSA JACKSON PERSON

Flight Attendant/Flight Leader with Delta Airlines in
Atlanta, Georgia

I was blessed to meet Joan Hunter at one of her Healing Conferences. I was inspired by her testimony of overcoming betrayal in her first marriage and how God was using her life for His Kingdom around the world. In 2002, a lady said to me, "One day God is going to use you. You are going to travel to many cities and many places. Your testimony will be used, and you will touch many lives." God has confirmed the same word several times over the years through different people. I knew God would bring it to pass. In 2007, after my husband left me for another woman, I decided to pursue a dream that God had placed in my heart many years ago. This job took me to places I had once prayed about going.

After meeting Joan and hearing the similarity in our testimonies, I knew that I wanted to be involved in Joan Hunter's ministry. In February of the next year, I received an e-mail about Joan's Healing4Haiti mission. I felt that it was something God wanted me to do. Because it was during a holiday weekend, I knew it would take an act of God for me to get the time off from work. Yet in faith, I began to prepare as if I would be going on this mission to Haiti.

I went to her website, filled out the necessary paperwork, and mailed back the forms, and things began to come together. I sold magnetic beaded bracelets made in India for $10 to pay for vaccines, meds, and supplies I would need to purchase for this trip. I wrote letters and spoke with some of my friends who then committed to donate to help fund this mission.

For work, I bid my vacation to have the time off and did all I could to clear my work schedule until April 10th. When our schedules came out on the afternoon of March 19th, I was disappointed to discover that I had been given two trips during the same week I was planning to be in Haiti. I believed God had placed this passion in my heart for Haiti, yet in the natural, it looked like I was not going to have the time off. I placed my trips on the eCrew Swap Board in hopes that someone would pick them up. Days passed and I was still scheduled to work the same week I was going to be in Haiti. I began asking God, "Did I miss You? Did I not hear You right?"

In the following days and weeks, God gave me reminders from co-workers and others who would speak to my heart—gentle words such as *faith* and *perseverance*. This was a constant reminder that He placed in my heart.

Until the evening of Monday, March 29th, I was scheduled to work on April 2nd. I was supposed to fly to Port-au-Prince the next morning! That same evening I went to run errands and get last-minute supplies I would need for Haiti. I believed God was going to work it out somehow, but I had no idea how. I had done all that I could. I had talked to other flight attendants about the mission. I had raised money. I was able to get rid of one trip by taking on another co-worker's scheduled "On call days." Still, I had one trip that remained on my schedule. Finally, I had to surrender it to God and simply say, "Lord, I cannot do this. I need Your help."

That evening I checked my e-mail. There was a short message from my manager that read simply, "I have given you the time off. Best wishes in Haiti. Call me when you return!" As simple as that, *God* had taken care of it! I shouted in my car; I praised Him; I cried tears of joy. I was literally blown away by God! He had come through for me again.

Hope, Healing, Power... For Me Too!

Once in Haiti, I made friendships that will be forever engraved in my heart. The team consisted of 36 people who came from various places, yet there was such unity while we were in Haiti. Everyone on this team brought something special to this mission.

It was so beautiful to see and experience the Body of Christ with different gifts working the way we did together, with one purpose in mind. I felt so unworthy to be called and to be used, yet God placed me in Haiti for such a time as this.

During our trip, the anointing power of God was unlike anything I had felt in my life. We came to bring love, hope, and the healing power of Jesus. Yet I was the one who also received each of these things and much more that week. I had been injured on an aircraft, which left me with very bad back pain. I had never had any physical problems in my life, yet I found myself on pain meds, in physical therapy, and many mornings not able to stand without pain. I had been seeing a specialist for over four months when, after several visits, he wanted to give me spinal injections that he said would stop the pain, but there were no guarantees.

I knew there must be another way; I thanked him, but declined. I decided I would wait; I knew that God could heal me. And what did God do? He healed me. Several of the women on our team prayed for me, and since then I have had no pain in my back despite my physically demanding job that requires me to do a lot of standing and lifting. I left all the medicine I brought with me in Haiti!

It was very difficult for me to get on a plane April 6th. While many of the team members flew back to Houston, I was going back to Atlanta. It felt like half of my heart was somewhere else. I did not realize how much I loved not only the people of Haiti, but also each of the team members God had placed together during that week.

Radical Change

I shed many sobbing tears on the plane to Atlanta. A lady whom I sat next to held my hand and we prayed passionately together for healing to come to Haiti. I felt the pain and loss they had experienced, and my heart literally ached like no words can adequately describe.

Days after coming back to the U.S., I knew that this trip had radically changed my life, my outlook and passion in life. I have a new passion and purpose. I believe part of this passion is for the healing power of Jesus Christ to be known to all. I once read that it is not the "position" that matters in life, but rather the passion that counts. God has given me such passion for Haiti. I will always remember the more than 350,000 orphans who often do not have one meal a day and do not know what it is like to have water. We are called to take the love of Jesus and the healing power of Jesus to Haiti and the world so that the blind will see, the deaf will hear, and the lame will walk.

CHAPTER 20

THE HARVEST OF A SEED

BY MARCUS DAVIS

*Employee of Hunter Ministries and Joan Hunter Ministries
from Kingwood, Texas*

With no plan to be part of the Haiti mission trip, but a desire to see the Lord do great things, I had been asking the Lord what His part was for me. I hadn't heard the Lord speak anything to me specifically, but in a meeting with Joan Hunter, my heart leaped within me to do something and to do it *now!* I called my wife and told her that the Lord had spoken to me to sow a seed into Joan Hunter Ministries in order to be a part of this mission. Of course, my wife said I should do it!

We were hoping that we could do much more, but at the time we only had $200. I wrote the check as quick as I could and went back to the office to find Joan. My wife and I wanted to be the first ones to sow seed toward her ticket to Haiti, knowing that God was going to do great things. I was amazed when she told me that we actually were the first ones to give toward her trip, but I knew that we wouldn't be the last. God was going to pave the way for this trip because Joan was being obedient to His call to Haiti.

When I put the check into Joan's hand, she said, "We were talking about you last night and want you to go to Haiti with us as a representative of Hunter Ministries, if the funds come in." I immediately knew that the Lord wanted me to do more than just sow into the trip. But did He really want me to go? My wife and I began to pray more intensely about the steps that we would have to take in order for me to go. I had never been out of the country before; therefore, I did not have a passport.

At that point, it was about two and a half weeks before the ministry was to leave, and I was not prepared at all because I had not planned on going. The next day I decided to begin the process of getting my passport at the local post office. I knew that I didn't have any time to waste so that morning I was praying that the Lord would guide my every step. I wasn't sure of the process or how long it took to get a passport, but my guess was more than two weeks. I was right; the man working behind the counter said it could take up to six weeks, but if I paid the extra fees, I might get it back in three weeks.

I wasn't sure what I was to do. I thought, *Lord, I am not 100 percent sure that I am going to Haiti, so if I am to go, You will have to do a miracle.* I told the post office worker that I wasn't sure what I needed to do, but I knew that I needed to pray for direction from the Lord. I went out to my car and called my wife to tell her all that had happened and ask her to please pray with me because I wasn't sure what to do. As I hung up the phone, I began to pray, and before I said five words the Lord spoke to my heart to go back in the post office. I grabbed my Bible and went back in, thinking that I would read my Bible until they opened up the passport line.

As I was standing in the back of the post office, a lady came up to me and said, "I overheard your conversation with the clerk about your passport. If you send it off here, you won't get it back in time." Then this lady began to tell me who to call and where to go to get the passport quickly. I was so amazed that the Lord sent this woman to me to give me the answers that I needed that I said to her, "Thank you so much. You are an answer to my prayers. I was just praying outside in my car that the Lord would help me, and He sent you!" I don't think this lady knew the Lord because she began to quickly walk off, and I said to her again, "no, you don't understand, *you* are an answer to my prayers!"

When I left the post office, I called the phone number the lady told me to call and they told me I had to make an appointment. I had to bring my driver's license, my birth certificate, and my airplane tickets in order to get my passport from them.

I said OK and I hung up the phone, saying, "Lord, this will show me if You really want me to go or not. There is no way I could have my tickets in my hand in this short amount of time unless it is You."

That was on a Monday; the next Saturday my wife and I were at home praying and worshiping the Lord when my phone went off. I got up to check it, and it was a message from Joan saying, "We have the space and the finances for you to go if you still want to go." This included my airplane ticket! I looked at my wife and said, "Honey, I am going to Haiti."

I called and made the appointment, and within 24 hours I had my passport in my hand! I sowed a $200 seed, and God made a way for me to go on a mission trip that cost over $2,000. Wow, what a harvest!

Right Where He Wanted Me

This was my first mission trip so when we got on the plane in Miami, headed for Haiti, a little fear tried to come on me. My thought was, *This mission is too big for me.* As I sat in my seat on the plane and looked over at a Haitian man across the aisle from me, a great love came over me for the Haitian people. All of a sudden, I felt like I fit in. I was right where the Lord wanted me to be, and His grace was already at work.

The first few days in Haiti were amazing. The first day hundreds of pastors from all over Haiti came to the training sessions and they were hungry for the Lord. I watched as Joan poured into them and our ministry gave out hundreds of sets of *How to Heal the Sick*. I was so touched by the love of the pastors and unity that they had with each other. Pastors from every denomination came. It showed me that when we are desperate, no denominational wall can keep us from getting what the Lord has for us.

One Scripture that describes our mission is found in Matthew 11. John the Baptist was in prison and sent his followers to ask Jesus a very important question:

> ..."*Are You the Coming One, or do we look for another?*" *Jesus answered and said to them, "Go and tell John the things which you hear and see: 'The blind see and the lame walk; the lepers are cleansed and the deaf hear; the dead are raised up and the poor have the gospel preached to them'*" (Matthew 11:2-5).

That is exactly what we saw over the next few days. I prayed for a little boy about eight years old who was deaf and mute, and God totally healed him, and he heard and spoke for the first time. As we were praying for people, I could feel the compassion of Jesus flowing through me. People would surround us, pull on me, and say, "Please pray for me and my family."

God shattered the work of the devil in Haiti, and we were there to help them shake off all that oppression. Our team worked together in unity; we were truly working together as one. After the services we would all gather back at the mission house and share awesome testimonies and then we would get together and pray. Although most of us had never met before this trip, we worked together and prayed together as if we had known each other our whole lives.

My life will never be the same again. I told my wife, Alisha, that I felt like God had enlarged my heart with His love for the world and especially for Haiti. I can't wait to return and see all the things that God spoke through Joan and our ministry team come to pass.

Challenged by the Contrasts

Returning to America, after such a trip to a country that has such great need, changed the way I think about everything. Just the other day our ministry was having a foot washing service and someone commented that the leftover water after the foot washing was cleaner than most of the drinking and bathing water in Haiti.

The mission trip has given me a greater appreciation for the blessing that I and my family have in America. I was amazed that, although many had nothing, they had more peace and joy than most Americans who seem to have everything. The pastors, with the little resources that they had, had greater vision to reach their country than most pastors whom I have met—most of whom had fairly unlimited resources. Although the American churches have so much to offer to the Haitian churches, the Haitian churches have a lot to offer to the American churches also. What the Bible states is so true; we truly are one in Christ, and we need each other. I am looking forward to returning to Haiti to continue the work that God has begun through Joan Hunter Ministries.

CHAPTER **21**

THE SEASON TO TRAVEL

BY SUZETTE FEARS

*Minister of Music at Love in Action Church and a Lay
Chaplain at Methodist Hospital in Houston, Texas*

After I ministered once at a men's shelter 15 years ago, a young
man came up to me and prophesied that I would travel around the
world with a healing ministry. I must have had a skeptical look on
my face because, at the time, I had two young children and had no
desire whatsoever to travel. He then said that when it happened,
I would remember the prophetic word given to me. Over the last
three years, God has faithfully confirmed that word. In January of
this year, I asked God what was on His agenda for me. He replied
with one word: *travel.* So when Joan sent the e-mail a month later
about Haiti, I knew it was the answer to the voice of God.

Although I knew this was God's plan for me, I had no idea where the money was coming from. One Wednesday night, the pastor took an offering for Haiti. Another major ministry was sending relief funds, and he wanted our church to partner with them. I had $100 in my purse for another expense, and the Lord told me to give it to the Haiti fund. I named that seed "Haiti trip." I asked the Lord to supply every need for my trip to the point of overflow.

Two weeks later the first $600 was due. It happened to be pay day! My husband and I agreed to sow that money out of our household budget and asked God to replace it. I began to seek God about where my harvest was.

He impressed me to send out mission letters to my friends and family. I sent out letters to about 50 people. Two days later a sweet missionary responded that she would gladly give $100. I knew her funds were limited because she recently had heart surgery and had been unable to minister. She promptly put it in the mail, or so I thought. A week passed without receiving it, and I began to take authority over the devil. A few days later, her letter appeared, and the $100 she sent had multiplied. She sent me $200 instead!

The same day a dear friend of mine whom I worked with years ago sent $100 in the mail. Three days later, my mother-in-law gave me $500 right before the last installment was due. Two days later at church, my pastor announced that the church was giving me $1,000. Wow! God paid for the trip and then some! It's so interesting to me that I sowed $100 and all the gifts I received were multiples of 100. The measure you use to give really is the measure God uses to give back to you!

Blessed by the Unexpected

Haiti was not at all what I expected. I did see poverty, but I did not sense the hopelessness that I expected to experience. The people in the midst of the rubble were carrying on. There were small businesses going on as though nothing had occurred. The people's hearts were so eager and receptive to the healing power of God. Wherever we went, they wanted prayer.

At the healing service, after Joan called for ten people to come forward with pain and she demonstrated the power of God to heal them, people rushed to get in line. They were so hungry and so open to the power of God. As we laid hands on them, they received their healing with ease. A couple of people we ministered to received the Lord Jesus and the Holy Spirit. Hallelujah! Also there was a sense of freedom and restoration from the past and freedom from poverty. At the end of the service on the last night, the people rejoiced with singing and dancing. The presence of God just saturated the atmosphere.

The best part for me though was what I considered "the bonus." The Holy Spirit imparted to the ministry team three times while we were there. I thought that was so sweet of Jesus to pour into us even though our mission in Haiti was to pour out to the

Haitians. One night Paulette Reed flowed in personal prophecy to each person on the team. The word that was given me was so special that it has stirred a new hunger in me for the glory of God. The next night, the Holy Spirit equipped us with special tools that we needed to accomplish His plan for our lives. The night before returning home, Joan imparted an apostolic anointing to those who became a part of the Alliance. Wow!

Singing in the Hospital

Since returning home, the anointing to pray and sing over the sick has increased. I go to the hospital weekly to pray for the patients. The other day, I encountered a patient who was moaning loudly in pain. As I started singing, the presence of the Lord filled the room and he was immediately freed from pain. Glory to God! I also have a greater boldness to pray for people wherever I am for whatever their need may be. I believe that this is my season to travel. I am available to God to go wherever He desires.

CHAPTER 22

SOWING REVIVAL

BY PASTOR PHIL HALL

*Senior Pastor for Impact International Church of
Denver, Colorado*

I spoke with my wife, Mary, recently about how this trip happened. We started to recall all the little things that occurred and how the Lord called on me to make this journey.

I received a text message from Joan on Sunday, January 17th, saying that she would be in Denver services at a metro area church and telling me that she hoped to see us there. We joined Joan for the Friday night service and God did mighty miracles. As we pastor a church here in Denver, we were on our way to our own Saturday evening service when I got another text message from Joan. All the text message said was, "March 30 - April 6

Port-au-Prince, Haiti. Train n equip pastors then healing crusade. Restoration n hope to Haiti. Joan Hunter"

Mary and I both got excited for Joan and offered to support her trip from our church funds. I thought that was going to be it. We both heard from God, and that was what He told us to do. It was settled. We went to support Joan's Sunday services, and it was during the Sunday evening service that the atmosphere began to change. I am not someone who just up and decides to make a journey outside the country. It has only happened twice, and both times it was because God started dealing with me about going. Mary and I made a mission trip to Costa Rica in 1998, and I made a pilgrimage to Israel in 2007. In both cases the Lord dealt with me during a church service, telling me that He wanted me to go.

During the Sunday evening service preliminaries, Joan invited Brother Bill Henderson from Colorado Springs to the platform to talk about the planning for the trip to Haiti coming in late March. Brother Henderson said that God was looking for a few good men to make this trip. My wife, Mary, said to herself, "My Phil is a good man." The Lord spoke to her and reminded her that she had mentioned earlier that day how we should be watching our budget. He told her that I would not talk to her about going on the trip after having that talk unless she brought it up first.

I was sitting there listening to Brother Henderson, and I started to get that burning knowing in my spirit that had happened in 1998 and then again in 2007. God had His hand on me, and as I have heard preachers over the years say, you can be sure when "you know in your knower." I knew in my knower.

About that time Mary turned to me and said, "Do you want to go?" I could only look at her dumbfounded. She asked again, "Do you want to go to Haiti?" I could barely get out of my mouth that the Lord had just spoken to me about going. Of course, I was concerned about the finances because we had talked earlier in the day about that very issue. I told Mary that we would have to depend on God for the resources, but I knew that He wanted me to go.

Mary and I walked with Joan and Curtis out to their vehicle after that Sunday night service. I told Curtis that the Lord had put going to Haiti on my heart. I left it at that, but God does demand commitment. After Joan left Denver, going to Haiti kept coming up in my spirit. The Lord continued to deal with me. Finally on Thursday afternoon, January 28th, I sent Joan a text message. "Hi Joan, could you use help in Haiti? I have a valid passport. Phil."

Exactly one minute later she responded, "Yes. I will send you info as I get it."

I sat in my office stunned. This was going to happen. Down in my spirit, I was dealing with being a good steward of my finances. The Lord told me to look at this as an investment. Blessing would result! A week later we received a large and unexpected refund check from the IRS. God had shown up again, just as He had for my two previous trips. The money for the trip was there! God is so good, isn't He?

It was different this time, though. I knew this trip was something big with God. God has a plan for Haiti just as He has for each of us. God wants souls! God wants Haiti! Haiti, a country that twice has dedicated itself to satan to obtain power. Haiti, a country that lives in abject poverty. Haiti, a country sorely in need of a loving and forgiving God. Haiti, a country about to be cleansed by the fire of God! God is about to do something *big!* A nation will change. A people will change! Can you hear that heartbeat? It is the heartbeat of God pursuing a people.

Torches in Haiti

Tuesday, March 30, all 36 of us arrived in Port-au-Prince, Haiti. We stepped off the airplane into heat and humidity. It was 95 degrees, and you could cut the air with a knife. There was chaos all around us. Skycaps tried to grab the bags out of my hands to make a couple of dollars, pushing each other out of the way to get at us and our luggage.

The next day, we all went to a private outdoor meeting center to train pastors and leaders from all over Haiti. The Haitians were very hungry to see the things of God. They crowded up around the platform to see legs grow out. I prayed with a Haitian pastor who had lost one of his three daughters in the "event," as he called it. Trauma, stress, and the spirit of grief left him and his whole countenance changed as we prayed.

There were 13 men on this trip, and we met every evening to pray and fellowship. That Wednesday evening God gave me a word, "We are sowing exactly what we will receive while we are here in Haiti. We are sowing revival in Haiti. We will take revival home, wherever home is." The Lord gave me a vision that I shared with the men that evening as well. God showed me torches being lit in Haiti and the fire of God sweeping across Haiti! The torches are the Haitian men and women involved in the training and the three-night crusade that would follow!

It was not long before I began to see the initial fulfillment of the word God gave me about sowing in Haiti and taking revival home. The second day of the pastors' training was the beginning of a new direction for me and for our ministry. The Holy Spirit spoke to me several times, telling me that I will preach in Haiti and that He is connecting me to Haiti. I never expected to hear that, but I am excited to be one of the torches lit on fire for God in Haiti.

After the training was over, the next day the team traveled to a local Port-au-Prince hospital to minister to the sick. As we waited for a translator to go with us into the men's ward, I met a young couple who had come to visit their aunt in the women's ward. She had been injured in the earthquake. I offered to pray with them, and the husband responded that they were Christians. I told them, "What a coincidence! I am a Christian also!" They looked at me like I was nuts because they thought I wanted to lead them to Jesus. I asked them what Jesus could do for them. I asked them what needs they had.

They told me that they had been unable to have children so I laid hands on them for healing and prayed for the wife specifically. The husband is a preacher and heads a Christian school with 60 students. The people in his village make fun of him because he is depending on God instead of going to the witch doctor and getting the voodoo to work for them to gain what they want. I broke the word curses off him and his wife and then prophesied "multiplication, multiplication, multiplication" over them. God told me to tell them that they will have many children! The Lord allowed me to minister to that young man for such a long time that the other team members had to come get me when it was time to leave.

Deliverance in the Streets

The Friday night healing service was the most exciting service I have ever experienced. We were right across the street from the Presidential Palace that now lies in ruins. The worship was beyond anything I have ever experienced. Hundreds of thousands of Haitians sang about beating the devil up, kicking the devil out of Haiti, and pleading the blood of Jesus over Haiti. The spot where these meetings were held is the same spot where, for many years, the voodoo priests would come to make blood sacrifices. Now, it is being used to glorify God and welcome the freedom won through Jesus' blood sacrifice on the cross!

People pushed up against the barricades with looks of desperation, determined to break through for prayer. One young man wanted prayer for his stomach, but kept holding his hand on the left side of his chest. Another wanted prayer for lower back problems. A middle-aged man had a knee that allowed the lower part of his leg to shift around in the socket. Laying hands on him, I could feel the knee snap back in place under my hand and asked him if he was healed. The man would answer "no" through the interpreter. This continued on a number of times; each time the knee would pop and the man would say "no!" I finally had to ask the translator to find out what was going on here. He said the man was saying "no pain!"

Finally, a young man came over for prayer. He needed prayer for "a bad spirit." I asked him if he wanted to receive Jesus as his Lord and personal Savior. He did. After he accepted Jesus, I commanded the demons to come out in Jesus' name. That young man had pure joy on his face! This was one amazing night! Every one prayed for received a healing from Jesus!

The next day, the team spent the morning at a flea market held at the United Nations compound. A lady was so touched with the blessing she received from the Lord that she gave me a brand-new shirt and a pair of trousers. I accepted her gift and later donated the clothing to Pastor Rene's ministry.

That evening's crusade was very unique. People received salvation. God healed backs, headaches, and stomachs. Then toward the end of the service, one of the women on our team called me over. She was in a panic. She had started to pray for a woman, and the woman had started to howl and scream. She was manifesting! Walking up to the woman, I slapped my hand on her head, and shouted, "Come out in Jesus' name!" The demon began shouting and screaming! The woman's body began to sway and jerk. I was very persistent. I kept my hand on her head, pleading the Blood of Jesus. I said, "The Blood of Jesus compels you; come out!"

The woman dropped to the pavement. She began to violently shake and tremor. Her body arched up. Every time I said, "the Blood, the Blood, the Blood," the demon would howl and then scream. The woman rolled over the pavement and I maintained contact. A young leader for Pastor Rene and another young man ran over to assist me. They put their hands on her as well and began commanding the demon to come out with me. The young leader said, "It is the spirit of voodoo! Call it by name!" I commanded "voodoo" to come out in Jesus' name! A couple of minutes later the demon came out. The woman was set free. She began weeping and shaking my hands and thanking me and thanking Jesus, and then walked off a different person.

More and more people came up to me for prayer. I laid hands on a blind man who wanted his sight back and said that he "hurt" all over his body. I laid hands on his eyes for some time. I prayed for his body and all the pain left him at once! I asked him if he believed Jesus would heal his eyes. He said he did. I told him to confess daily, "Thank You, Jesus, for healing my eyes." I made him commit to it. He told me he would and gave me a big hug with tears running down his face. God did a healing in every one!

On Easter Sunday, Jesus showed up in a mighty way. The Sunday night service, the final service of the Miracle Crusade, was one to remember. An elderly woman had both her ears opened and she could hear clearly. She then wanted her sight back in her right eye. She believed Jesus would do it for her. I laid hands on that eye, and she received her sight! This went on for 30 minutes or so. I was then called for by Kelley, Joan's husband, to come pray for a man at the platform. This man was claiming to have demons. He didn't have demons, but I had him recommit his life to Jesus Christ. Seven more people lined up right behind him.

They either recommitted their lives to Christ or received Him as Lord and personal Savior for the very first time. What a service!

God did a mighty work in Haiti! Haitian radio even said that these meetings were the biggest thing to hit Haiti since the earthquake!

Reaping Revival at Home

As I mentioned earlier, while the team was in Haiti, the Lord gave me a word, "We are sowing exactly what we will receive, while we are here in Haiti. We are sowing revival in Haiti. We will take revival home, wherever home is." I came home expecting God to do great things in our church here in Denver. God is faithful!

I want to make it clear. I didn't join this trip because it seemed like the right thing to do. I didn't go to Haiti because of the necessity to help people who were in need. Those things are indeed important, but in order for me to leave my family and our church, I had to hear God say He wanted me to go. He made it plain to me. When Joan first mentioned going, it wasn't clear whether we would be sleeping outdoors in tents or just what the circumstances would be. Knowing this and hearing from God, I knew I needed to be obedient. Obedience with a right heart is the door to unparalleled blessing.

After arriving home, I noticed increased blessings for our inner-city church. A number of people had new jobs. The people were prospering. We've had a worship leader for a number of months now, but he always had to use recorded music for the service. The day I got off the airplane on my way home from the airport, our worship leader called me and told me that we had someone who had decided to play piano for our worship services.

What a blessing he is. He comes with over 30 years of professional music experience! The presence of God is very strong in our services and growing stronger week by week.

I am amazed by what God is doing. The presence and the power of God have increased greatly in our services. There is a tangible difference in my preaching, teaching, and prayers for the sick. When God gives me a word, the anointing runs through me like electric fire. So great is our God! In just this past month, God has also created new connections for us with people whom we just find amazing to be in contact with. The promise of God came home with me! God is greatly moving in our ministry and in our church. I look forward to every opportunity the Lord is providing.

All of this has happened in just the first month that I was home. I know in my spirit that revival will be a reality. It is what has been my heart cry since we started the church 19 months ago. It is coming! The manifest power of God is increasing! God is blessing us greatly! I recommend to every pastor to step outside the box. Be obedient to what God calls you to do. It might not be convenient at the time, but you will not be able to outrun the blessings of God as a result of your faithfulness.

CHAPTER 23

HE LOOKS FOR WILLINGNESS

BY TRACIE WINEGAR

Waitress from Houston, Texas

After the Haiti earthquake, I cried for three straight days. As I started to pray for the people of Haiti, I saw myself under the rubble with them. So when I read the e-mail from Joan, everything became so clear to me. I was supposed to go to Haiti. The Lord told me that He was giving me a heart for Haiti and that's why He allowed me to identify with their suffering.

As soon as I sent in my request to go, the enemy said to me, "What do you have to offer? You are a waitress who's going with people in ministry." Then my Father God told me that He was not looking for experience, but willingness. I was so honored and excited to go, but I was still nervous at the same time.

I have sponsored a girl in Haiti for five or six years now through Compassion International, and I remember looking at her picture once and telling my friend that I would *never* go to Haiti because of all the voodoo practices that go on there. Little did I realize that the Lord was preparing me to go the whole time. The Lord led me to start studying the spirit realm about eight months before the earthquake. God is so good! He knew that one night during the crusade I would need that knowledge to pray for a young teenage girl who was oppressed by demons. Greater is He who is in me.

Thankfully, I did not have to worry about my finances for the trip. My friends and family gave me around $700, and then my tax return took care of the rest. Thanks, Uncle Sam! Thank You, Jesus!

Nothing but God

When I arrived in Haiti, I really didn't know what to expect. When I was 18, I went to Mexico City after the earthquake in 1985, but I had never seen poverty like I saw in Haiti. The Lord started moving the day we arrived. What a feeling to know that Father God had picked each and every one of us to be there. Not only was He moving on the people of Haiti, but on each of us also. We all felt close to each other right away. We all began to realize that we were part of something very special.

I can't tell you how many people came up to me while we were in Haiti and asked why we were there. When I told them that we were there for them, to pray for them, it was so unbelievable. They were so touched and so grateful. Each day my spirit woman grew stronger and stronger.

While Joan was teaching the 700 pastors how easy it was to pray for the sick, I just stood in the back of the tent to watch and listen. It was so cool to see their faith grow and grow as they understood what she was teaching them. They got it! It was so exciting to know that they were taking this back to their villages, churches, and families.

Each night during the crusade, as we prayed for more and more people, my own faith grew. I can't put into words what it felt like praising the Lord with thousands of Haitians who had just lost everything but God. It was something I will never forget. I can still feel that amazing feeling right now. They know how to praise the Lord!

Going to the hospital and the orphanages was so special. I prayed for every child I touched. We all knew that we were God's hands. A friend of mine took up a collection at work and raised $350 and then put in another $300 of her own to buy supplies for the orphanage. The bag was packed full of medical supplies, baby stuff, and general hygiene items. I thought the doctor at the orphanage was going to cry when I pulled out that bag and gave it to him. He told me that it was an answer to his prayers. What a wonderful feeling to be able to see the smile on his face. This whole experience was amazing, but I think the most special thing for me was leading so many people to the Lord. They were so hungry for Jesus.

No Longer Timid

Since I have been back home, I have been telling everyone who will listen what Jesus did in Haiti. I was so excited to walk up to a neighbor who does not believe in God and tell her about the thousands of miracles that took place. No one will ever be able to say in my presence that Jesus Christ is not alive and working miracles. I no longer feel timid about asking people if I can pray for them.

I prayed for a man whom I was waiting on in the restaurant the other night. He was from New York and in town getting cancer treatments. I told him what happened in Haiti and asked if I could pray for him. He almost leaped out of his chair as he said "Yes!" Thank You, Jesus.

If it was up to me, it would be mandatory for everyone to go on a mission trip in his or her lifetime. You always hear that it changes people, but you really don't understand till you actually experience it yourself. I know that this is not my last mission trip the Lord is going to send me on. He gave me a servant's heart, and I want to serve. I am ready, Lord!

CHAPTER 24

ON TOP OF THE MOUNTAIN

BY LAURIE COTTON

Eddie Bauer, LLC Store Supplies Coordinator from
Amanda, Ohio

On July 1, 2003, my mother had the first of three strokes. I took time off from church to take care of her and never went back to church. By 2007, my mother had recuperated enough that she could drive three miles to her church, but still I did not go. In March 2009, I returned to my church and felt I was home at last. The week I returned, Joan Hunter came to conduct a healing service. I went to all the services that Joan led. Soon after Joan's visit, I began healing classes under the instruction of Mike and Cindy Teagarden. I attended the series of healing classes twice. Soon after graduation, I joined a healing team.

I am hooked! God has done so many healings and miracles through me despite my faults. I also do photography and video for our team. Our team was led to fast for direction for three weeks in January 2010. While on this fast, God led me to pray for the people of Haiti. My heart so ached for these people. In February 2010, our team was informed that Joan Hunter Ministries was planning a trip to Haiti. My spirit leapt when I heard the news of the upcoming trip. However, I really did not think that I would be able to go. My mother does not do well when I go on vacation.

I am a single parent of two grown children who still live at home. I am still paying part of their expenses while they are paying on their education loans, so I live paycheck to paycheck. I had no way to raise the money and very little time. The amount of money needed seemed like a mountain that would take forever to climb, and I did not have enough time to climb it (or so I thought). I began praying as if God would have me go to Haiti. I felt I was to go, but it seemed like there was no way.

Then I found out that I would be receiving a bonus—my first bonus in three years. I planned to buy a camera to replace my current outdated camera. Then a few days later I found out my friends Kim and Daron Mosley were going on the trip to Haiti. I asked how much the airline tickets were. When I heard the cost, I also heard "Your bonus is for Haiti." My bonus was almost enough to pay for my flight to Haiti. I knew without a doubt that I was to go to Haiti and that God would provide.

I e-mailed Eric Cummings asking if there was room for me to go with the Healing4Haiti team. He e-mailed me with the criteria to be approved to go to Haiti, also stating that there were only one or possibly two spots left for the trip. I met all the criteria to go on the trip, and I even already had all of my immunizations. I then e-mailed my pastor and asked for his blessing to go. Within seconds, I had an answer from my pastor. He would send me to Haiti with his blessing.

I e-mailed Eric with the good news, and he told me to go ahead and book my flight. My friend Kim booked my flight for me, and it was $100 cheaper than I thought it would be. Thank You, Jesus! I also was able to travel on the same flight as Daron and Kim, so I would not have to travel alone.

On March 14, we were informed that we needed to pay $600 in two days. On March 15, I found an insurance check that I had lost for almost a year. I was able to pay the money on time. God is so good and always on time! I waited until March 21 to tell my mother; I hoped to avoid her getting upset or sick. In the past my mother would have been worried about me, and she would have made herself sick over it. To my amazement, she was perfectly fine with my going and was excited to hear about all God would do while I was in Haiti. She was proud that I was going to help the people of Haiti heal.

This was a miracle all on its own. I have never missed an Easter with my mother or children. Mom always insisted that my daughter and I prepare an Easter meal for the family. But this time my mother had peace about my going and being away for Easter. I knew, that I knew, that I knew, that this was God's plan for me. This put me on the top of the mountain, so to speak.

The Sunday before we left, my church gave me just enough money to pay for my food to and from Haiti and a couple souvenirs. What a blessing! God truly provided for every detail.

He Cares About the Little Things

Wow, the trip to Haiti was indescribable. Our flights were all on time, and we met the team in Miami for the short flight to Haiti. We arrived to extreme heat and a band playing Caribbean tunes. The images on television do not compare to the actual devastation you see when you step out of the airport. There is so much debris that it seems almost unfathomable that it could ever be cleaned up. The people seem to stare as if they will never recover from shock. As we traveled to the epicenter of the earthquake, the devastation grew worse, and fewer and fewer buildings were still standing. There was more garbage, and the stench was horrible. The tent cities and people seemed to multiply also.

We originally thought we would be sleeping on the ground in a tent city with no water to wash. However, God sent His angels before us and provided more than we ever imagined. I arrived at the house we would stay at with apprehension and anticipation. The house was fenced in with cement blocks and razor wire and a big red, locked, uninviting metal gate with a dog lying outside.

We walked through the gate to see this huge, beautiful house. The inside of the house was big enough to house all 36 members of our team, Pastor Rene, and his staff. We all had our own bed to sleep in, cold water to shower every other day, two meals a day, and much more. I brought food with me to eat because I am a very picky eater, but there was not one meal prepared for us in which I did not find something I liked. We even had Domino's pizza a couple of nights. Pizza is my favorite food! Our God is an awesome God!!

We were in Haiti during the rainy season. Before leaving home, I prayed for blue skies and big white fluffy clouds and mild temperatures. The temperatures were hot, but not unbearable. It rained the first two nights we were there, which actually cooled it down for sleeping. We had blue skies and big white fluffy clouds the entire trip. God even takes care of the little things. I would wake up early in the morning sometimes before anyone else to go to the roof to talk to the Lord and take pictures. The sunrises were beautiful. I had my own little sunrise service with God on Easter morning. *"I watch, and am as a **sparrow** alone upon the house top"* (Ps. 102:7 KJV).

Loving on Haiti

There were many opportunities for the team to pray for and love on the people of Haiti. Joan taught a group of pastors how to lay hands on the sick and pray for healings and miracles. These pastors were so hungry for the tools we had to give them. God worked mightily those two days. There were men putting tile on a roof who were dancing on this sloped roof with raised hands, praising God. They were not part of the seminar. They had holes in their clothes and no shoes on their feet, yet they still praised almighty God.

As we prepared to minister to the people during the three-day crusade, the multitudes grew. *"And great multitudes followed Him; and He healed them there"* (Matt. 19:2 KJV). The praise and worship began and the people gave all they had to worship God. They were hungry for God. We prayed for many people and saw many miracles before our eyes. God healed people of headaches, stomachaches, parasites, heartache, infections, and skin diseases. There was a man who had been deaf since birth. I prayed for him and within a few minutes this man was jumping up and down praising God. He could hear for the first time in his life. It is such an incredible feeling to know that God can work through me to perform the miracle to heal a deaf man. A woman who had a stroke came through my line. She could not move her right arm or right leg, and she could not speak. After I laid hands on her and prayed, she was walking, raising her hands in praise, and shouting, "Merci, Jesus!" Thank You, Jesus! *"He sent His word, and healed them, and delivered them from their destructions"* (Ps. 107:20 KJV).

We visited a hospital and prayed for the patients. We held the babies and loved on them. A little boy named Yazi was visiting his mother who was in a body cast. Yazi's mother told me that he had been buried in rubble for five days with no food or water after the quake. When he was rescued, he did not have a scratch on him. He was a perfectly healthy little boy.

We traveled to the country to see an orphanage and school. There were hundreds of children who came to the school just for a bowl of hot porridge. There were only about 40 students enrolled in the school. Most of the children were not in school because their parents could not afford to pay. The company I work for donated t-shirts for me to take to Haiti. Some of these were handed out to the children at the orphanage. It was a wonderful day.

The children loved the attention. I normally have my hair pulled up in a bun on the back of my head. One of the girls motioned for me to let my hair down, so I did. Some of the children were amazed that the length of my hair was six inches above my ankles. They were mesmerized. A couple of the girls rubbed their hands through my hair. They thought that hair as long as mine must have hair extensions and that made me laugh.

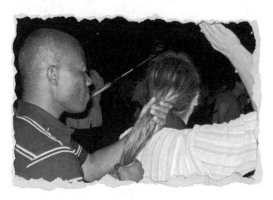

Pastor Rene Joseph also has a rock crushing and block making facility on the orphanage property. One of the guys in our group explained how to make the concrete stronger so the new buildings will not crumble in the event of another catastrophe. Also, houses are being built and the people are given the opportunity to start businesses and to buy the houses at a low cost. This was a wonderful day.

On our last day, we went to another orphanage. We visited 29-30 children three years old and under. Most of these children were HIV positive. Our group loved on, played with, and prayed with these children. They clung to each of us, and we did not want to put them down or leave them. A daughter of a co-worker had sent care packages of toothbrushes, toothpaste, dental floss, and Band-Aids® with me. These were delivered to the orphanage for the children to use.

Planning for Next Time

I returned home a changed person. It is very hard not to think of the people of Haiti. I close my eyes and see those sweet little faces that need someone to wrap their arms around them and love them. I think of the people in the tent cities, of those who have parasites and broken hearts. These people have lost everything and think they have no hope. They need God in their lives, and they need their land to be healed. I see things on sale at the store and buy it for the next trip. I am thinking of how to raise money for upcoming trips, but I know that my ways are not always God's ways and that He will amaze me over and over again. I know without a doubt that this was just the first of many trips.

My mother was so excited to hear all the things that happened in Haiti. She told everyone she met and had me pray for her friends. She received prayer several times, but she did not feel it was her time to be healed. On April 26, my mother went on to be with our Heavenly Father. Now she is completely healed never to be in pain again. I cannot begin to express the joy it gave me to hear my mother bragging about how God had used me in Haiti.

To think that I almost gave this trip up to stay home to take care of her is inconceivable. She would not have wanted me to do anything different. I thank God that He provided the way and used this humble spirit to fulfill His will.

CHAPTER 25

FORWARD INTO DESTINY

BY TIFFANY KING

Personal Assistant from Nashville, Tennessee

I almost didn't come on this trip because of money. I hadn't been working as much as I would have liked. I just didn't think that I would be able to make it happen. I told God that if I was supposed to go, He would have to provide. A close friend of mine gave me money before I committed to going. Later several other people made donations that covered my expenses for the trip. I'm so thankful that God provided.

Beyond Amazing

Haiti was such a life-changing trip for me. Over the last ten years, I have participated in many mission trips. This trip to Haiti has by far had the greatest impact on my life. To witness hundreds of thousands of people being set free and healed was beyond amazing. I had the opportunity to pray for a woman who had a huge rock fall on her face during the earthquake. Her face was swollen and parts of her cheekbone were chipped. I prayed for all the pain and swelling to go and for her cheekbone to be restored. Immediately all of the swelling and pain left and her cheekbone filled in. A few minutes later, a woman who had lost her left breast and was in a lot of pain came to me for prayer. God suddenly took away all of her pain, and as she was rejoicing, her breast grew back!

One of the hardest moments I have ever experienced happened at a hospital we visited in Haiti. I walked into the maternity ward and noticed a woman who was watching us as we prayed for the mothers and their babies. As I walked over to her, she motioned for me to pick up her baby girl and said something to me in French. As I reached down, a mother in the bed next to her translated that she wanted me to keep her baby. She wasn't married and had lost everything in the earthquake. She didn't think she had anything to offer her baby. I told her that I could not keep the baby, but instead prayed that God would restore to her what was lost in the earthquake. Not only did we pray for the material things, but also for God to show her how to love her baby and how to be a godly mom to her daughter.

Such Boldness

Upon returning to Nashville, I was invited to speak at a young adults meeting. I was able to share about our experiences and to pray for everyone there. Everyone who had a need was healed. God also stirred and imparted a desire in me to move in our community, and He created a stronger passion in those who were there.

Since this trip to Haiti, I have lived my life with greater passion and fulfillment, knowing with confidence that God has ordered my every step and that every day I am living in God's will for my life. God has given me such boldness! Friends who have known me for years have noticed how much more vocal I am and how much more passionate I am. I have always been passionate about helping widows and the orphans, but since I visited Haiti, I have focused my energy on serving others. It's not just about going on a mission trip for a week; it's about living your everyday life in the mission field in your neighborhood, your office, and your family.

Since returning from Haiti, my life feels like everything is falling into place. Before going to Haiti, I sold my car because of costly repairs. For two months I waited to even look for a car, knowing that I needed to get a car within my budget, but I was not finding anything I could afford. I knew that God has called us to be faithful with what He has given us. I knew that if I listened to Him and was patient, He would provide. I had been seeking God for direction, not only just concerning a new car, but for my entire life. I wanted to know His plan for my life. I prayed for direction and all the while did odd jobs just to make ends meet.

After two months of being patient, I found the perfect car. It's everything that I ever wanted. I've also been offered an opportunity to travel and assist in coordinating several overseas mission trips. These are just two examples of direct answers to prayer. I have wanted to travel and help coordinate mission trips for ten years. I often wondered why the timing hadn't worked out and why I was still working in an office instead of working with orphans. Now, I see that it was God's hand working everything together for my good. He was putting things in place, bringing relationships together, and developing a fully obedient heart in me. Now is the time for all of the waiting and praying to turn into action! Because of my obedience to serve in Haiti, God has made this my time to be moving forward into His purpose and destiny for my life.

CHAPTER 26

PERSONAL RENEWAL

BY MIKE HARRIS

International Evangelist with Ignite Ministries from England

When the earthquake hit Haiti, I just prayed, "Lord, I would like to help in some way," and then I left it in His hands. A few days later, I received an e-mail from Joan inviting me to join her. I thought to myself, *If my wife, Janice, says I can go, I will go.* When I asked her a few hours later, her reply was, "Yes, you can go as long as all the money comes in and does not affect the family income"—which meant that God had to make it happen. I gave her a big kiss and then e-mailed Joan to tell her that I was coming, even though I didn't have a penny at that moment in time.

Over the next six to eight weeks, all the money came in. One of the churches I minister in gave me a large gift. Also a lady in my office makes wonderful cakes, and she started baking and then selling them to everyone in the church—well, almost everyone—and raised almost £200 for my trip. I had an opportunity one Sunday morning for ten minutes to show a video on prayer and fasting in Haiti and to talk for a few minutes about what I was going to be doing. Afterward so many individuals came up and gave me money to help with the trip that I had enough money with me to help the people of Haiti. All the money came in for the flight and insurance as well, and I was able to take along over £1000 to help the people. What an amazing God we serve!

Revitalized and Encouraged

There is so much to tell about what happened while I was in Haiti; it could become a book in itself. The past two to three years have been a really hard time for me—I had to step down from ministry for a few months, as well as move out of the family home for a year. My wife, Janice, and I were having some issues we needed to sort out, but before I went to Haiti, I had already been back in the home for over 18 months and God was rebuilding our marriage.

For me, personally, I felt I needed to be around anointed ministry to help kick start me once again. All through these past few years I have never doubted God and my calling, but when you are being hard pressed on every side, it does knock you around a bit. Also, during this time I have been facing illness within my own body, and ministering to yourself daily with no real improvement can also affect your confidence. I had the opportunity to minister to others who had much worse conditions than me and see them be healed. I felt renewed and encouraged. My faith and expectation has risen with a fresh excitement and confidence in God to fulfill His promise and calling for my life.

This man could be the next president of Haiti.

I ministered to a number of people who were all healed and set free from the influence of voodoo. Dumb spirits were cast out. One lady who said that she had a snake inside her was set free. A man totally deaf in both ears could hear, the blind could see, and the lame walked. None of this was a surprise to me, but it was really great to get back into the flow of the anointing again.

This young lady was totally blind, now she can see!

While I was in Haiti, I also received a prophetic word from a lady who has an amazing prophetic gift. The word refocused me back to the time before all of the difficulties I faced a few years ago. Over these past few years, I had begun to get a bit hard-hearted and cynical in the way I talked and ministered to people. The Lord was encouraging me not to be hard, but meek and tender-hearted to those around me. This tied into another word I had received before I left for Haiti. I was told that I had allowed calluses to appear on my heart, but the Lord would remove them as I let Him.

This lady could not walk at all, but now she can run!

While in Haiti, I also became the first overseas member of the 4 Corners Alliance, which I believe is very significant. The alliance is an apostolic covering for those who want to be a part of the healing ministry that Joan oversees. I believe this will open new doors and opportunities for me within this nation and also around the world.

Change in the UK

Since I have been back in England, some things are beginning to change. Praise God! Over the past few years, the healing ministry within the UK has taken a bit of a knock, with many churches not wanting to get involved in this kind of ministry because of what has been happening on television and how some people have conducted themselves in public. It seems that anyone who has a healing ministry is being tarred with the same brush. However, God is still on His throne, and I know things will turn around as more and more miracles occur.

Since returning from Haiti some new ministry opportunities have come my way. I am training a group of evangelists in how to reach their community in a greater way. I have a healing school booked for later on in the year and a three-day conference on how to sharpen your axe head. This will teach people how to use the gift they have to reach the people they meet with the healing power of Christ. I also have a few healing meetings booked in other churches over the next few months.

At the beginning of 2010, I felt the Lord wanted me to hold my own healing meetings every other month. These are slowly growing and the number in attendance doubles each time. At one of these meetings, as the band led us in worship, the anointing and the presence of the Lord just entered into the room. It felt like you could almost reach out and touch Him. It was as if the dove had just settled on each of us in a very gentle but real presence of God. When I began to minister on Matthew 12:20—*"A bruised reed He will not break..."* (NIV)—I could just see people receiving the Word into their spirits. Many came forward for ministry. A lady who suffered with vertigo for many years was totally healed; her arthritis and knee pain were gone. A young mother had a tumor in her brain and was afraid to go to the doctor. While praying for her, I felt the fire of the Holy Spirit pouring into her head. She gave her life to Christ and said that now she would go to the hospital.

Since returning from Haiti, I also ministered to one man who has cancer. He is receiving chemo every other week, but he does seem to be getting stronger each time we pray together. I am expecting God to totally heal him. A lady whose lower spine was crumbling was also totally healed and all the pain left.

CHAPTER 27

"HAVE FUN"

By Linda Adkins

Decorator, designer, event planner, florist, landscaper, cake decorator, and retired hairdresser and wig stylist from Pasadena, Texas, who previously traveled with Joan Hunter for six years

Our Lord has given us so many beautiful places on this earth, and I have traveled to some of them. The only place in the world that I never wanted to go was Haiti. I could handle Russia, England, Africa, almost anywhere, but never Haiti. Why? My feet did not belong on soil dedicated to the enemy! However, someone had other plans for me.

My friend Joan told me that she and her team were invited to go to Haiti to minister. All of a sudden I felt something go off inside of me. I knew I wanted to go. What was I thinking? *Not Haiti!* I was happy and excited for her and those who would be going. Would I be one of them? I didn't know for sure because of the expense. Like a lot of people, I didn't think I could afford to go. My husband and I had a trip planned to celebrate our 40th wedding anniversary. We still didn't have enough money for that, so how could I go to Haiti?

I knew a lot of people were asking for donations from sponsors, but I didn't feel that was the right thing to do. Time was too short to get an extra job, so I just prayed and felt that if God wanted me to go, He would make a way. I spoke to my husband about the money for me to go, and he said he didn't know. We agreed to pray and seek the Lord. We both wanted to be in His perfect will.

Later, my husband, Kenneth, asked me if I really wanted to go. I told him I believed this was what the Lord wanted me to do. He told me if I really wanted to go, he would sell some of his retirement stock. This would provide the money for me to go to Haiti. The only hitch was that there are restrictions on when he can sell his stock, and the time it takes to get the money can sometimes be delayed. But through God's faithfulness, I had the money in less than two weeks.

As I was telling people about my trip, many of them said, "You will never be the same." I knew I would be changed forever, but I didn't really know how. One of my sons said, "Have fun!" *Have fun?* What was he thinking? How could I have fun on this trip going to a country so devastated? But I did; I had the most wonderful time in my life!

The Most Beautiful People

Soon I was on a plane with 35 other team members headed for Haiti. Like everyone else, I saw the devastation, the mountains of rubble, the smell of death in the city, the tent cities, and the hopelessness in the faces of the people. People were struggling everywhere. I saw a person jump in front of our bus trying to die. I saw people in a hospital that was very primitive by our standards. I saw orphans in the country and in the city. I saw what looked like a hopeless mess!

I also saw the most beautiful people I have ever encountered! They had suffered so much, not just from the earthquake, but from centuries of all kinds of abuse. I just kept seeing beautiful people. First, there were the pastors, who were hungry for the goodness of God to share with their churches. Then there were the people wanting healing, both physical and spiritual. So many would come up and say, "I need Jesus," or "I have a devil in me; I need Jesus!" When an interpreter wasn't available, the people would put our hands on their bodies where it hurt. We watched their faces as the Lord touched them and took away their pain. We watched as they were set free and as they accepted Jesus as Lord and Savior. We saw smiles, peace, and brightness in their eyes where darkness had been moments before. Trauma no longer had a hold on them.

For me, the second part of the trip was forming new friendships with my team members. I never dreamed I would meet such wonderful people. I should have known that if they were all friends of Joan Hunter, they would be special! We shared rooms, showers, food, roller coaster bus rides, and our feelings. It was wonderful. I thought we were just going to be a blessing and minister to the Haitians. I was not expecting so much personal ministry from our Lord. But God let us know that He had hand-selected each one of us for this trip. We received personal prophecies and spiritual gifts from Heaven. We felt His tangible presence the moment we gathered in the airport, and it did not leave the entire trip.

How can I explain how my personal family grew by 35 in just seven days? Where are the words to express the love, the kindness, and the joy? Is this a small taste of what Heaven will be like? I am overwhelmed by the love I feel for the Haitian people and my new family as I write this.

Many Good Memories

The moment the plane landed in the U.S., I knew our American soil felt different. I know why people kiss the ground when they arrive in America for the first time. I also said, "I never, ever, ever want to leave our great country again."

Then I heard the Lord say, "Linda...."

"Yes, Lord, I didn't really mean that." I would be going again. Not only to Haiti, but to all of the other countries He has lined up for me to visit. He only wants the best for us. It is not always close to home. It is not always easy, but it is always His best.

As the days go by, I miss so much. I miss our bus rides and Mono our driver. I miss the people; I miss the food and our "house." I miss hearing the men pray and sing on the porch late at night. I miss my friends and the beautiful Haitian people. I don't miss the roosters crowing all night, though!

I have great memories of the Haiti trip. I will always remember the little boys and girls placing my hands on their stomachs and the children wanting us to take their pictures. They always loved to see themselves in our cameras. They all wanted to hold our hands. People were dancing and worshiping for hours, their faces full of joy. One man and woman wanted to be set free and have children. I will always remember the woman whose face had been burned beyond recognition. She had no eyes or nose; only her mouth wasn't scarred. I had no interpreter, but somehow she understood. She was free! We all have so many good memories. Thank You, Jesus, for allowing us to go to Haiti with You!

CHAPTER 28

A STEPPING STONE FOR CHANGE

BY LORI GUNNELS

Accounting Clerk from Tomball, Texas

When you know that you know that God is involved, everything just flows together. That is how it was for me when the Haiti trip was first mentioned. I knew I was called to Haiti, and I knew He wanted to go with me. I have often joked around that God would have to send me a flashing neon sign as confirmation for certain things, but He didn't have to for this one. I simply knew. God is good.

When I stepped out in faith for this trip, I had two major concerns: one was finances and the other was my daughter. I am a single mom with an active teenage daughter. What do I do with her while I am across the world? Who will take care of her? How will she get to school and other activities? Again, let me say that God is good and that He takes care of the details.

The weekend I was scheduled to be gone, my daughter had two school holidays and a weekend. One of my best friends lived about five miles from the high school and offered to watch my daughter that week and transport her to and from school and to and from softball activities. What a major blessing! My daughter was completely taken care of while I was away on my Father's business.

As God took care of my daughter, He also took care of the finances. We needed approximately $1,600 for the entire trip. God created rivers of abundance that flowed my way. Thank You, Jesus. I only provided $100 of that money. God did the rest.

My secular employer gives to a lot of charities so I thought it wouldn't hurt to ask if the company would help sponsor me. Goodness, what a river from God! My employer sponsored half of my trip! Hallelujah! God also moved on the hearts of three co-workers to help me go to Haiti. I believe they were making a deposit in their Kingdom account and storing up treasures in Heaven. Thank You, Jesus, for letting me be a vessel for their blessing! Two of my friends blessed me too. Not only did one of them watch my daughter, but she also helped sponsor me. I had several friends support me with supplies that the Haitian people needed. My whole family sent up to Heaven prayers of protection, prayers of blessings, and prayers of guidance. God showed Himself as Jehovah-Jireh to me on this trip. He is truly my Provider, and I will be forever grateful and honored that He chose me personally to tend to His sheep. *Amen!*

Loving the Children

I did it! I got my first stamp in my passport! Hallelujah! I participated in my first mission trip! Hallelujah! And for the first time, I truly walked with God. Thank You, Father! This trip was awesome, to say the least. It was incredible to see so many miracles jam-packed into one week of God-ordained appointments.

It was the children who won my heart in Haiti. The day we went to the hospital, I really didn't know what to expect. All I knew was that I wanted to go into Labor and Delivery. God heard me, and God granted me favor. Joan and a group went ahead while the rest of us were waiting outside. But the wait was not long for me; Joan sent for me and, sure enough, I was going to Labor and Delivery with the *babies!* Oh, how my heart rejoiced! I walked up, but Joan stopped me, prepared me, and then released me to pray. What I witnessed was shocking to me. My heart felt a void as much as my eyes saw the void.

I am used to seeing every type of machine in hospitals in America. We have every medicine, cleanser, and comfort we could ever think about and need for birthing a baby or two. What I saw in that room consisted of people, babies, tables, and beds. I did not see one piece of equipment that hospitals normally use. There were approximately 15 families in this room. It's hard to imagine that they labored, delivered, and recovered in this one room. Most of the time when I was in that room, I felt like an intruder. I wondered what the parents' thoughts were regarding us being in there with them. Some of their eyes had no emotion; some had hope.

I was able to pray for three of the babies. One in particular was a preemie. That baby was just wrapped in a towel, lying by the mother—both were just staring into space. I prayed life into that baby. It hit me hard that in America we would immediately stick a preemie in an incubator for several months, but in Haiti it was wrapped in a towel. However, I know the words I speak to God are much stronger and more life-giving than any incubator in the world.

I was able to speak with one of the mothers; she was the only radiant mother in that room. She told me her daughter's name was Zoe, and her son's name was Emmanuel, and she proudly proclaimed that she was a Christian. I smiled and told her Zoe meant "God life." I have always loved that name for girls. I then prayed life into that baby girl. She was round and cuddly with clear skin—absolutely gorgeous; you could already see God in her.

The group then journeyed to the infant/toddler room. I made the rounds, touched a few through their cribs, and prayed Jesus over each and every one. The last one I stopped by was a baby boy with big, brown eyes. I picked him up and immediately he snuggled down into my chest. I felt his fever, prayed over it, and soon felt the sweat from the fever breaking from him. He lay still in my arms, full of peace and calmness. Thank You, Jesus. I have to say that that was enough of the hospital for me. I did what He needed me to do, and I was ready to leave.

At the Sunday evening crusade, God gave me the most humbling memory I have of Haiti; He brought me face to face with two teenage boys. Through the interpreter, I learned that the first young man was an orphan; both of his parents had died in the earthquake. My heart broke and cried silently to God, *What would You have me say to him?* His family was lost from him forever; where would he go? How will he live? Who will be there for him as he grows into a man? I remember I had to pause, take a deep breath, and lead him to Jesus. I had the privilege of leading him in a prayer of salvation. I also prayed God's protection over him, and he seemed deeply touched.

Then his friend quickly stepped forward. He too was an orphan. That night he met Jesus for the first time. I felt God had something special for him; I felt God say "Prophet of God," and He wanted me to pray that into existence. Never having done that and not knowing how to do it, I simply prayed and called that forth in the young man's life. God is going to do tremendous miracles through him for Haiti. I guess this memory is so profound to me because they were teenagers. I have a beautiful teenage daughter, and I could not imagine life without her, nor could I imagine her having a life without a mom.

I loved visiting the orphanages. I loved seeing the children. I was truly in awe of them because they were so happy and filled with joy and laughter. It was as if they didn't know how poor they were. We are all called to be childlike. The children loved having their pictures taken. They would pose, smile, and then rush to see the digital screen, and then they would all fall into hysterical giggles. I laughed right along with them. I could have stood there all day hearing their giggles. One little girl stood out in my eyes. She had on a white dress and had the cutest smile and the brightest eyes—but it was her little girl giggles that shook me! I wanted to do whatever I could to keep her giggling. I wanted to take her home with me because she was precious beyond words.

These children are my memories of Haiti. Yes, the miracles were unbelievable, but it was the children and the babies who made a lasting impression on me. It's the laughter I keep hearing; it's the hope in their eyes I keep seeing. I pray His protection over each one. I pray His angels to stand guard over them and preserve them in purity and love for His glory. Now that I am home, I still think of the children. I still see the faces, and I still feel their hands holding mine. I want to go back just for them.

Seeing Myself More Clearly

God has shown me a few things about myself that have been hard to face. He is changing me little by little, bit by bit. To be frank, He has shown me that I am selfish; I can't think of any other way to describe it. Most of what I do in how I treat people, in how I talk, in how I act, has been my "flesh."

In Haiti, I saw how people lived, and I thought of how I live. I have had to struggle all of my adult life raising my daughter as a single parent, scrounging for money to pay for school lunches and wondering how the bills were going to get paid. I also had all the pressure of protecting her and teaching her about life. In Haiti, they had the same struggles as I have, but in a different and greater magnitude. God gently showed me that I should have done this for this person in kindness, but I didn't think of it. Or I should have said one thing, but my tongue was a bit sharper than necessary. I have been humbled in this envisioning of my heart. I try each day to open my heart a little more, to say something kind to someone or to be a blessing to someone. It's not an easy task to change an old mindset and break habits.

I believe I have gotten a little bolder too. Before the trip, I never had the courage to walk up to people and pray. It used to paralyze me with fear. Within the first week back, I walked up to two people and prayed with them. Thank You, Jesus. Hopefully, their healing manifested. I don't know because I didn't stick around long enough to ask.

Finally, I know part of what I am supposed to do. I am going to build orphanages here in America. Of course, I will help international orphanages, but I want to build them here in America. I have the name already for these homes. It will be a raising, educating, and loving family environment for children who have no hope in their eyes.

The first Scripture God ever gave me was Philippians 1:6: *"Being confident of this, that He who began a good work in you will carry it on to completion until the day of Jesus Christ"* (NIV). I know in my heart this trip had a certain purpose for me. I believe it was a stepping stone for God to continue changing me from the inside out. God used this trip to put a desire in my heart and usher in the Prince of Peace to the people of Haiti.

CHAPTER 29

SUITCASE FULL OF TOYS

BY DIANA RADABAUGH

Ordained Minister and Founder of Because He Lives Ministries from Elkhart, Indiana

It is said in the circle of believers that God will not call you without making the provision to go. My confidence was in Him, and many gave so that I could be a part of this wondrous adventure, the Healing4Haiti trip.

The first time I heard about the earthquake in Haiti, my heart went out to the people. "Dear Lord," I cried, "they are under so much already with all the spiritual warfare and poverty that they fight. Oh Father, help them. Oh God, heal them." Everyone with a heart prayed, fasted, sent money, and sent help in whatever way he or she could. Deep in my heart, I so desired to touch them, hold them, look into their eyes, and love them in Jesus' name. I sent money over and over again to different ministries that were on the scene, but that wasn't enough. I wanted to be there to hurt with them, cry with them, and bring them comfort.

Through the years, 24 years to be exact, I have had the blessed opportunity to work with Charles and Frances Hunter. I traveled with them on 39 mission trips all over the world. Then God started calling me to go on my own, and I have been to many crusades of my own. The desire to go to Haiti was nurtured through many other mission trips, but none pressed on me like this one. When I heard the word *Haiti*, I would cry out, "Please, Father, let me go for Your Glory; let me go."

One day when I was on Facebook, I noticed that my friend Debra was going to Haiti. I called her right then. She told me that she was going with Joan Hunter Ministries and encouraged me to contact Joan. I called and spoke with Joan about going to Haiti. She said, "Yes, of course," and my prayers were answered!

Three weeks before we were to leave, I became very sick. I never get sick. It has been years and years since I have been ill. I got my shots for Haiti, and a couple days later I was in bed. In prayer on that Thursday I told the Lord, "If I am not better by Sunday, I am going to have to cancel." That night I received an e-mail from my granddaughter Mariah. "Nanna, can I send with you some of my stuffed animals for the children there in Haiti?" With tears I said, "Yes, honey, you can." Soon after that, Sara, her sister, wrote, "I am so happy to be able to give some toys to the children. I am going through them now." Then little six-year-old Jenna Lee, their baby sister, wrote a note to the children of Haiti to be included with the toys she chose to give. In the note she said, "I was so excited when I heard that my Nanna was coming to Haiti because then I knew that now I could help too. I hope these toys make you smile." When I read that, I said to my husband, Jerry, while sobbing, "Only Jesus will keep me from going to Haiti. I have a mission with these toys and the children."

With a very special little black suitcase full of toys and my luggage, I was on my way to an answered prayer to be with the people of Haiti. In Miami I met up with Joan, her husband, Kelley, and the rest of the team. I can barely remember that meeting because I was sweating and praying for strength. And just as you might expect, somewhere between Miami and Port-au-Prince, Haiti, the Lord God healed me completely. He is so wonderful!

Touching Hearts

On January 12, 2010, all hell broke loose on Port-au-Prince, Haiti, when a 7.0 earthquake exploded under Haiti. About a month before we arrived, President Preval called for three days of prayer and fasting for the nation rather than having the Carnival, an ungodly Mardi Gras-type of event that they have every year. Instead the president asked that the people pray, fast, and call on a righteous God to help their homeland—and the prayer meeting was held in the same location that we used for the healing meetings just a few weeks later. The president broke down and cried during the prayer and asked God to help and bless his country. He repented for his country's voodoo and witchcraft and asked God to take control of Haiti. There were reportedly a million people at the prayer meetings, and it was also declared that over 100 voodoo priests were among those who gave their lives to Jesus Christ. Many pastors and leaders were there to lead the country into repentance and to receive the blessings of the living God.

While we were in Haiti, every day was full of activity. We went to Sugar Cane Museum for two days. Joan did such a superb job of training pastors and leaders. She answered many of their questions and trained them to pray for the sick. They were like innocent children, yet mighty warriors of faith. She laid hands on everyone to impart the anointing. It was beautiful to see all the pastors and leaders stand around the edges of the park as Joan laid hands on them.

During the Healing meetings, God put it on Joan's heart to break trauma off of the people. I could feel in the spirit the relief that the people experienced. The pressure, the fear, the sorrow, the sadness left as the spirit of trauma was commanded to go in Jesus' name. The miracle services were tremendous. The praise and worship was electric. Everyone praised the Lord with all that was within them. It was wild.

When Joan came to the microphone, the crowd became quiet and listened very intently. Have you ever heard a hush come over one million people? It spoke loudly of the presence of God. Many were healed. His healing virtue touched all who reached out to receive it. When Joan prayed, the teams and others were released to pray also. Before we finished praying, those being prayed for would receive their miracle.

There was one young woman about 22 years old who was in severe pain. Her left arm had been broken by the earthquake. Her flesh looked like it had been burned. Her pain was intense when she tried to lift her arm. One of the other team members, Debra, and I prayed for her for 15 minutes. Debra said, "The Lord is telling me to hold her." So she did. It seemed like five minutes or so. It was love that melted the unbelief, pain, and fear.

With every prayer, the huge knot in her arm got smaller and smaller. The knot felt like cement; it was five or six inches long and three inches wide. After we would command and pray, she would take her hand and grab mine and put it on the wound to show me it had sunk. As we prayed, the knot got smaller, but the pain wasn't gone.

At one point the Lord said, "Now her fear is gone." I looked at her face, and it instantly changed right before my eyes. Her appearance completely changed from darkness into light. She glowed, and she lifted both arms in the air rejoicing, praising God, and thanking Jesus for His miraculous, glorious miracle! She was healed. All glory to God!

There were so many miracles and healings. However, the greatest miracle of all was that people came up to me at the meetings saying, "I need Jesus. I need to get saved." We spent Easter Sunday celebrating the truth of the Resurrection of our Lord Jesus Christ by doing the Kingdom work.

One day we had the chance to go to a local hospital to pray for people who had been injured by the earthquake. We had to go into the hospital in groups so as to not overwhelm them. I saw a young woman standing a few feet away. I walked over to her, not thinking about the language barrier. I said to her, "Hi, where were you at the time the earthquake struck?"

She answered me in perfect English and said, "I was sleeping in my room with my cousins. One was on a cot against that wall. My other cousin and I were in a bed on this wall. The earthquake came and the wall broke away and my cousin rolled down in a crevice as the second floor fell into a hole. I never saw her again."

I hugged her and we cried together. Then I said, "Now you won't only live for yourself, but for her and the glory of God!"

She said so sweetly with great determination, "Oh I know; that is exactly what I am going to do." I don't think I will ever forget her beautiful, glowing face as she turned and walked into the hospital.

Toward the end of our time there, we were all deeply touched when we visited Pastor Rene's orphanage. We loved on the kids, played with them, and helped feed 500 precious children. We loved them and they loved us. Then we went to another orphanage for babies and toddlers.

One little boy about two years old came over to me as I got to the bottom of the stairs. He pulled on my pants, so I sat down against the wall and held him. He came into my arms like he had always been there. He let me hold him for the longest time. I just kept looking at him and humming "Jesus Loves Me." The lady who was a caretaker came over, rubbed his little head, and said, "He is one of our HIV babies." As soon as she walked away, I went to praying for this precious baby boy.

I suppose I could go on writing for a very long time. We all learned so much from the Haitian people. It was a privilege to serve them.

CHAPTER 30

INCREASED ANOINTING

By Mike and Cindy Teagarden

Founders of Teagarden Deep Water Ministries and River Valley Life Center from Lancaster, Ohio

We were checking the weather on the television when we heard the news that Haiti had been devastated by an earthquake. As Mike saw the suffering, the Spirit of God rose up in him and he said, "If You will send us, we will go!" This seemed impossible in the natural.

The Healing and Miracle Schools that had supplied much of our income for a year and a half had stopped. Our ministry team of 14 had gone on a 21-day fast to hear the Lord for direction.

New Schools and a conference had opened up to us, but it would be a while before we would get any money from them. The Lord was supplying for our financial needs through gifts and temporary work, but there didn't seem to be any extra money and real estate taxes would be due soon. We had been planting financial seeds for that, believing that God would provide. The Joan Hunter Ministries Ordination was also coming up. Four members of our ministry team were to be ordained. Our friend Pastor Paul Bishop had volunteered to pay for our trip to the ordination, but that would not include hotel costs and other miscellaneous expenses. It seemed that several financial miracles needed to happen in a short time.

Then I received a text from Joan Hunter that said, "How does a healing crusade in Haiti over Easter weekend sound?" We immediately assumed that this was the answer to Mike's prayer, but we learned that we would have to cover the cost of the trip to Haiti. We said, "Well, if God wants us to go, He will work it out." We continued to pray and seek God's direction for the trip, watching our words carefully and refusing to get into worry or anything negative. And God supplied the funds for the trip. Praise the Lord!

Love Army

I felt like the army of God had invaded Haiti, armed and ready to pour out the unconditional love of God Almighty upon His Haitian people and watch them be transformed right before our eyes.

While in Haiti we trained and equipped the local pastors and leaders so they would be able to continue the ministry started by our team. They had already received hundreds of books and DVDs in French. During the first day of training and equipping the pastors, we were worshipping God when we noticed a young fellow on top of a steep roof making some repairs. He was dancing and worshipping God with all his might while he worked!

One morning while we were training and equipping the pastors and leaders, a young male reporter motioned for me (Cindy) to come closer. He leaned over and spoke in English and asked, "Did you come to Haiti just because you care?"

I said, "Yes!"

The young man said with a huge smile on his face and with such sincerity, "Oh thank you so much and God bless you!"

They are so grateful for those who love and care about them, and they are somewhat surprised that we would spend our money, time, and effort to help them just because we care.

We also had a three-day "Healing Explosion" where we saw the glory of God being manifested each evening with miracles, signs, and wonders. Haitians are exuberant, radical worshippers! Each night, as far as the eye could see, hands and faces were lifted up toward Heaven as they experienced God's awesome presence. People left wheelchairs and crutches behind as God healed their legs. Many Haitians were filled with the Holy Spirit and delivered from broken hearts.

During the services the children of Haiti waited in line for us to pray with them. We did not always have an interpreter with us, but the children rubbed their stomachs and touched their heads to let us know where they were hurting. We prayed for each and every one of them, commanding the spirit of trauma and fear to go, and Jesus healed them all. We gave them lots of hugs, which they so desperately needed. We also touched each child and declared that "everything our hands touch shall prosper." This is something that Joan taught us to do, and we know the Word works even after we leave and go back to the States.

Mike took many people through an effective technique called "Tissues for Issues" (a form of deliverance), removing "root causes" that can bring bondage and sickness. God gave this revelation to Joan, and she has graciously taught it to us. We use and teach this method in all of our Healing/Miracle Schools and have seen great and mighty works of God! It works every time!

I prayed with a woman who was walking on crutches who seemed to have had a stroke. I prayed very specifically and asked her to say, "Thank You, Jesus!" I asked her to do something she couldn't do before. She did; she began walking without her crutches as we watched over her.

We also prayed for a lady in a wheelchair. After she said, "Thank You, Jesus!" we asked her to express her faith by getting up and walking, and she did! We walked along beside her the whole time for safety precautions.

Another woman who couldn't walk was sitting on the ground because she did not have a wheelchair. Mike and I prayed for her; then we helped her up off of the ground and had her say, "Thank You, Jesus!" to receive all of the healing that Jesus already paid the price for at Calvary. She began to walk!

Even with the 100 degree weather; dusty, curvy roads; men, women, and children bathing in small pools of dirty water; little pans for eating food; hungry dogs looking for food; and makeshift homes (tents and shacks) in row after row; I know we made a difference in the hearts and lives of many.

He's Here!

Since we returned to the States, we have noticed a change in our own hearts, ministry, and anointing. More doors have opened for Healing and Miracle Schools. We are flowing more in the gifts of the Holy Spirit and experiencing more of the manifested glory of God in our meetings. Our finances have also increased dramatically! Mike reports a special manifestation of the anointing at the beginning of every meeting. It's as if the Holy Spirit is saying, "I'm here. Let's go!"

CHAPTER 31

ONE MAN AND A VIDEO CAMERA

BY GEOFF MCCLELLAND

*Video Editor and Director of Photography for XP Media
from Maricopa, Arizona*

The Haiti trip, for me, definitely came about as a "suddenly" of God. I work for XP Media as a video editor. On February 24th I was on my way to meet my wife, Krista, during our regular lunch break. My cell phone rang, and I noticed the call was from Shirley Ross. Shirley is the producer of our television show, Extreme Prophetic with Patricia King. Shirley was away with Patricia at the time in order to visit IHOP in Kansas City. She had taken a high-def video camera with her in order to film some testimonies and footage of the revival there, so I wondered if she was having trouble with the video equipment.

"Hello?"

"Geoff, this is Patricia [King]. I'm calling on Shirley's phone because I forgot mine. On the flight to Kansas City I felt that we need to have a media presence in Haiti when Paulette [Reed] goes there with Joan Hunter. If you're up for it and OK it with your wife, with Paulette, and with Lorrie [head administrator of the XP media department], we'll see if we can get you in right away as it's already a couple days past the deadline."

"OK, I'm on it," I said.

About four hours later, Paulette had the flight booked, and I was shifting gears trying to get my head around the fact that I was going to be in Haiti in one month. The first thing I did when I got back to a computer was look up the location of Haiti on Google Maps.

As it turned out, Joan Hunter Ministries had been praying for media personnel to accompany the group and had reserved two spots for someone just like me. I had a different role from everyone else on the trip, as the type of ministry I would be doing would mostly take effect "after the fact." I had the job of bringing as much awareness of the trip back with me as I could to share with the rest of the world. It was a big job for one camera. When we shoot video on the streets in Arizona with a small ministry team, we generally cover it with two cameras. But now I had to cover the ministry of 35 other people with one camera. I just prayed that the Lord would guide me to the situations He wanted me to capture.

Hard to Imagine

To see the devastation from the earthquake firsthand was astounding. I'm not sure that it can be entirely represented on video. The dust, the stench of garbage and septic in the streets, and the spirit of despair can only be suggested through video, but to stand in the midst of it and experience it is almost overwhelming. I could only try to imagine what it must have been like on January 12 in Port-au-Prince when the solid ground began to shake so violently that buildings crumbled into a pile of rubble. It must have felt like the end of the world.

God was in the midst of our mission trip to Haiti. He provided us with food and water, beds, showers, electricity, international cell phone service, and even Internet connectivity only two months after the devastation. It wasn't quite the Ritz-Carlton, but compared to the conditions the Haitians were living in, it was the Ritz-Carlton. Hundreds of thousands of displaced Haitians are living in tents and will remain so for months—many for years—until the country is rebuilt.

God also connected us with influential pastors in Haiti. There is a good chance that one of the pastors we met will become the next president of Haiti, and another will become the spiritual leader of the country in Billy Graham fashion. We are praying to that end.

God moved mightily in Joan's services. But Joan's heart was to do more than minister healing. She aimed to impart and commission the local Christians to believe and walk in the promises Jesus established for all believers. We saw some instantaneous healings; we heard testimonies of healings that occurred later; and we are still believing for more healings to be completed.

After the concluding service on Easter Day, Pastor Rene's phone started ringing at 4 A.M. with radio stations wanting to interview him in regard to healing testimonies that were coming in. Some begged him to extend the crusade; others came from neighboring countries pleading with him to set up a crusade on their islands.

Rise Up into Fullness

If the video footage I captured only conveys one message, then I hope that message is that now more than ever there is a need for every Christian to rise up and live in the fullness of what Jesus Christ has restored to humankind at Calvary. If we could somehow grasp the depth of the power of the cross and the blood of Christ, we could plunder the kingdom of darkness by bringing literally billions of new believers into the Kingdom of our Lord in our generation.

CHAPTER 32

PRAY AND SEE

BY ELIZABETH TREGO

*Statistical Analyst, Analysis and Reporting for IHS/CHS
Fiscal Intermediary from Albuquerque, New Mexico*

On January 12, 2010, I was impressed to pray for Haiti. I, of course, did not know an earthquake was about to happen. I was stunned when I heard about the quake the next morning. God continued to put Haiti on my heart, and I was looking for a way to go to Haiti and minister. Our assistant pastor, Mary Dorian, said, "Let's pray and see what God does." Not a day had gone by before Mary called letting me know that had she received an e-mail from Joan Hunter about going to Haiti. Mary asked if I wanted to go with Joan. I said sure and asked what the dates were. I was at work when Mary called, and I immediately requested time off even though I did not know if I would be accepted for the trip or not.

God supplied all my needs right away. My church had a conference the week after I applied to go. We announced that I was going to Haiti, as if it was a done deal, and asked for donations for snacks and lunch during the afternoon break. Over $300 came in over that three-day weekend. Then my pastors, Wyatt and Claudia Moore, took another collection two weeks later and $600 came in. People also gave me Pentecostal handshakes (passing money to me through a handshake).

Marked by Worship

I did not know what to expect when I got to Haiti, but I knew God would show up because He wants to demonstrate His love to people by healing them and setting them free. Just going and being very dependent on God is one of the wildest things you can do. God will use you if you are willing.

It was the worship of the Haitian people at the crusade that has left its mark on me. A majority of these people were not baptized with the Holy Spirit, but they would ecstatically worship God. Everyone was thirsty, hungry, hot, and packed in like sardines—but that did not bother them. God does enjoy the praises of His people. The western world has nothing on these lovers of God. We barely get out of our pews.

I laid hands on people and they were set free from trauma, parasites, headaches, eczema, and back pain. I saw a young girl with a deaf and dumb spirit begin to speak on the last night of the crusades. It was incredible. Now I am planning on going back to Haiti and taking some others with me. Next time I hope to spend time in the streets with the people and visiting the smaller churches.

CHAPTER 33

ARMOR FOR BATTLE

BY SANDRA SHAW

International Evangelist/Missionary and Proposal Director
of BOLD Ministries from Stockdale, Texas

God is putting His armor on us. I saw this in the spirit. I also saw some of the Haiti team with three-foot metal snips in our hands. The armor of God is to protect us in battle, and the giant snips are for cutting off the chains of oppression. There were other tools that others carried into battle. Jeremiah 33:6 says, *"Behold, I will bring it* [Haiti] *health and healing, I will heal them and reveal to them the abundance of peace and truth."*

The first time I heard of this trip was during a phone call to Joan Hunter's office. Someone mentioned that Joan was going to Haiti, and my spirit quickened. I felt a strong manifestation of the Holy Spirit cover me from the top of my head to the tip of my toes. God was confirming that I was to go and be a part of this movement of God in Haiti.

Then an amazing series of events happened as I fasted for this upcoming trip. First, my daughter had a supernatural birth in comparison to her first birth. She had no pain, just pressure, and slept until the time to push. Second, both our sons decided to move closer home. One will help with the family ministry, which is an answer to prayer. And we will be able to spend more time with both of them. Third, our new ministry received its 501c3 non-profit status. It took a year, so this was a major step for our ministry. Fourth, unexpected ministry doors opened in several places overseas. It felt like God was confirming that we were on the right path.

As for the money, as churches found out about the trip, they donated funds. Many of these were small churches with less than 15 families—yet they provided funds for my Haiti trip. I also applied to the U.S. Census for a job. I tested, and they called and said I had a job, but not to expect a call for a month, which was perfect timing. I started shortly after returning from Haiti, and this temporary job brought in enough funds to pay off the Haiti trip and to provide for our next trip to the Philippines and Pakistan. God is good!

Lay Hands on the Sick

The first two days in Haiti were about training the pastors who came from all over the island. One pastor traveled 24 hours just to Port-au-Prince. They eagerly listened, but when Joan started to lay hands on people called forward for a certain health issue, they could not believe their eyes. They came out of their chairs, some rushing the stage to see more. Then they surrounded the stage out of curiosity. At the end of the first day, they left with anticipation of coming back the next day for more of God.

But I noticed that at the end of the second day, their bellies and their spirits were full. They left satisfied, knowing that there is hope in their situation and that things are getting better because they were not just given tools, but shown how to use them. The look in their eyes was different. They were committed to the birthing of a "New Haiti."

Then the three-day Healing Crusade started in the heart of the capital. Banners were hung throughout the capital city of Port-au-Prince to advertise the event. Trucks were also hired to drive throughout the tent cities proclaiming, "Jesus Christ is risen from the dead, and He has come to heal Haiti." When our big yellow school bus pulled up to the stage where loud speakers were playing music all through the capital, drawing in the people, it was a moment of anticipation for the whole team. Our excitement for what was about to happen was electric in the air. The team celebrated as the music played, the people came, and the miracles happened.

As Joan Hunter prayed over people on stage and they received healing, she would address the crowd, with Pastor Joseph Rene interpreting, telling them to place their hands on their own bodies and receive the same healing that she was praying for on stage. She told them that the healing power of God is there and that they could receive their healing where they were. As she would tell them this, they would calm down, knowing that they were all receiving healing. I watched as the masses would receive the healing.

Throughout the nights of the crusade people were prayed over. Here's a list of some that I saw: the blind saw (including a man blind most of his life), a lot of headaches vanished, and hearts that hurt were healed (they complained of a physical pain in their hearts, which was the trauma that Joan was teaching us to cast out of everyone). Those spirits of grief and trauma had to go!

The first night God brought me a Haitian man as an interpreter. He would explain in French Creole with motions, what they were going through; he could not speak English, but he followed me from person to person helping me. I would look into their eyes, seeing that their pain was gone and that they felt healing. Two young men wanted the baptism of the Holy Spirit. They pointed upward, wanting more of God, and they got it! I also prayed over stomachs, ankles, legs, knees, and a man with only one eye. I waited expecting to see the new eye, but it did not manifest at that moment. But believing for the healing is what is important—knowing that Jesus can and will heal. Remember, Jesus is the same yesterday, today, and forever (see Heb. 13:8).

Two young men approached me, one needing prayer for his ankle and foot, which were injured. We prayed and the pain was gone. I loved seeing the relief in their eyes. Then a little boy ran up to me and almost knocked me over, squeezing me so hard and giving me so much love it brought me to tears. He said, "I love you" in English. What a loving people!

Saturday morning we heard that a crowd of 250,000 had been there the first night. A Dutch and German camera crew was at the crusade. They interviewed Joan the next day and different members of the healing team. In Haiti, the next day, the Joan Hunter Ministries Healing Service was all over the news.

Saturday night there was a girl there who was having seizures. The crowd lifted her above their heads and moved her up to the stage. She was around ten years of age, and both of her parents had been killed in the earthquake. I had them hold the top of her body, while her legs hung over the barricade. She was totally passed out, but as I prayed over her, her eyes began fluttering. Then someone with security came and got her and took her on stage where Joan prayed over her, and she then woke up and was walking around. Praise God!

There was a beautiful little girl with one leg; her other leg was gone from the knee down. She saw the other children squeezing through the barricade and dancing with our team. I could see in her eyes that she felt so left out. No child should feel any rejection in a time of rejoicing and worship. She was heavy, but I picked her up and danced with her on my hip. She laid her head down on my shoulder. God's love was planted in the hearts of so many children and adults in Haiti. May it multiply.

There were lots of feet skin diseases. Two men took off their shoes to let me see their feet, and the skin was covered with a slimy clear coat of mucus. Without flinching, I put my hand on their feet because the Holy Spirit reminded me that *"they will lay hands on the sick and they will recover"* (Mark 16:18). The interpreter and the men were surprised, but I knew that God's Word is true! And they were healed instantly! As I took off my socks to hand to one man, they were saying, that's not the problem. I knew that, but I had many socks; this man had none. How fortunate we are in America. May we share our wealth with those in other parts of the world who are lacking.

Then my interpreter (this one spoke English) and I came up to a father holding his two-year-old daughter. He said that she could not see. I prayed, casting out the spirit of blindness and death over the eyes and speaking life into them. The father talked to the little girl; then the father started to smile. The interpreter told me she could now see. I kept looking at the father smiling a great big smile, and I kept saying "She can see! She can see!" I love doing the work of the Lord. Amen!

Easter Sunday was the biggest party that I have ever been to! They did not want us to leave! Amen! Haiti knows how to party for God! We got to go up on stage and dance and shout with the masses of people in the crowd. I thought to myself, *So, this is a glimpse of what Heaven will be like.*

I noticed in the pictures taken during worship and dancing with the children that many orbs had appeared. These round balls in the pictures are a manifestation of angels (see Ezek. 1). Angels were so thick in the pictures that it looked like snow was falling. Praise You, God!

As I prayed for a woman for lost memory to come back, she received tingling from the front of her head to the back, like a wave. I saw it in my spirit. When I asked if she had felt or received something, she confirmed it. I always remind people that it is the hand of Jesus touching them and healing them. It is not me; it is Jesus! One woman wanted to have more children. As I prayed, her hips rotated. I never told her flesh to move like that. This woman and many others were so receptive to receiving the healing that their flesh responded even before I spoke. It's all a God thing. Several people had loss of hearing in one ear; after prayer, they all responded that they could hear.

One woman whom I prayed over had lower back pain. After I prayed, she said she felt worse! My first thought was, *What would Frances Hunter do?* Then I realized that the spirit of pain was not listening and letting her go, so I got mad. I didn't look into her eyes like I normally do, but leaned over to her hips and commanded that pain to go in the *mighty name of Jesus!* It left! No more pain! She bent over and actually did a little dance as the power of God went through her body. Amen!

In all, about 1.2 million people were ministered to over the last three nights—and 600,000 to 700,000 were at the Healing Crusade on Easter Sunday night.

Such a Time as This

The Haiti healing team of 36 was reminded again and again that we were here "for a time such as this." In that same vein, the Holy Spirit impressed upon my spirit Jeremiah 33:6: *"Behold, I will bring it* [Haiti] *health and reveal to them the abundance of peace and truth."* This whole chapter in Jeremiah talks about the "excellence of the restored nation," and in many ways that was the theme of our time in Haiti.

One day after arriving back from a trip, part of the team went up on the rooftop to pray. It was amazing! We took pictures and then started to pray. I saw in my spirit a portal open from the heavens and angels came out in groups, side by side with long trumpets blowing announcing "God's Glory is here for Haiti, here to be released for such as time as this."

May we never forget the children who lost their parents and are now orphans in Haiti. There are several hundred of them.

And they are so thankful to get that one bowl of porridge—their only sustenance for the whole day. And here in America we all eat three meals a day; that has never left me. It was so clear to me that our work there was incredibly timely, and yet there is still so much more to do. I feel the Lord leading me to help find two cement trucks in America and ship them into Haiti to help Pastor Rene. I saw the location of the orphanage for the new orphans of Haiti. These men were digging in the hard ground with just shovels and using their hands to do all the work. This is not how it should be. I pray God's Kingdom people can come together and help these children and Pastor Rene's Helping Hands Ministry in Haiti. With God all things are possible. Amen!

I had my picture taken with a beautiful Haitian landscape on one side of me and a pile of trash on the other side. I came to stand in the gap for Haiti, to bring the hope of Jesus to Haiti. Each of the team members was handpicked to come to Haiti and handpicked for restoration. Because of our obedience, I believe restoration will begin in Haiti and in our lives as well. *For a time such as this!*

Emotional Healing, Too

Everyone had wonderful stories to pass around when they got back from Haiti. I did too, but I was so attacked by satan when I got back that it was not funny. Satan wants to stop any movement of the Holy Spirit, but if we surround ourselves with God's Word and stay close to Jesus, He will bring us through. My first month back was rough, and I needed to know that I was in alignment with God. As I sought Him, I felt Him reminding me of this truth.

I know that Jesus died for our sins (see John 3:16), and when I see the stripes on His back, I am reminded that He died for all sickness and disease (see Ps. 103: 3). But as a human who lives with emotions, I often forget that He was called a man of sorrows. He was rejected and despised; He was oppressed and afflicted (see Isa. 53:3,7). And according to First Peter 2:24, not only did He heal our diseases, but Jesus also took care of all negative emotions. I was reminded that I just need to live in forgiveness (see Ps. 119:133) and give all of my struggles to the Lord—and He will deliver me! Ministering is not without a cost.

We minister because of what we have been through. We know people can be set free because we have been set free. We must learn that Christ's complete work for us humans is for emotional healing, physical healing, and a complete spiritual redemption from sin. Psalm 50:15 says, *"Call of Me in the day of trouble; I will deliver you, and you shall glorify Me."* Life is not perfect, but where we choose to view it from makes a big difference. If we choose to stay in the valley, we are in the circumstance, but if we are on the mountaintop praising God, everything looks different.

I too was reminded to give it to God and watch God heal and restore what I could not imagine. No matter what the circumstance is, I will glorify My Lord and Savior. Satan will not stop me from answering the call of Christ.

Breakthroughs at Home

I started the job with the U.S. Census Bureau just two days after getting back from Haiti. This job has started many good things in motion and allowed me to complete some projects that will allow for more time with the ministry. Many doors of opportunity are opening for our ministry, and we are excited to see what God will do. I have been waiting on the Lord, and He just answered this morning, telling me that I am typing my testimony. I am realizing that our ministry is moving in a bolder direction, and I know that as I hold on to Psalm 138:8, the Lord will perfect (complete) that which concerns me.

CHAPTER 34

HEART'S CRY

BY DEBRA HOSKINS

*Founder of JC Ministries and Full-Time Itinerant Minister
from Standwood, Washington*

This was my first overseas mission trip, and the invitation came at a difficult time for my already full schedule. This was not something I wanted to take on, but God had other plans. You see, just a week before this invitation came, God gave me a repeated dream.

In my dream, I was standing in front of a half circle of men and women who were facing me. They were dressed in casual clothing and although I didn't see their faces, I knew they were ministers. I was handing to each person several tall, rubber-banded stacks of wallet-size prints of my watercolor painting titled "He hears your heart's cry." In the background I could see Haiti lifted up, as if it was hovering above the ground. I believe this is prophetic as God is lifting Haiti up out of the ruins. Just as the dream was ending, I heard my own voice say to God, "The people of Haiti just need to know that You hear their heart's cry." It ended and I woke up feeling my own heart cry for the men, women, and children of Haiti.

For several days I rehearsed this dream in my mind, over and over, trying to figure out how to go about getting that many prints made and delivered. I knew the cost would be great and pondered how to go about getting them to Haiti. I needed the blessed assurance that once they arrived in Haiti, they would actually get into the hands of Haitians. I knew only God could do this, so I laid it on the altar and rested in it, only to have the dream again—three times in a week.

Then it came as an open vision over my windshield as I sat in traffic, but this time I saw my feet on the dirt! It jarred me into reality. I immediately called a close friend, exclaiming, "If I get asked to go to Haiti, I am going to pass out!" That very night at the midnight hour, 12:24 A.M., I received an e-mail from Joan Hunter asking me to be part of a team going to Haiti!

My spirit was thrilled because God had brought me right back to the dream. I knew this was God, but my flesh struggled with the idea of actually going myself. This was not at all in my plans, believe me! So I thought if my husband, Jerry, would discourage me from going that it might be a little easier to just get the prints made, somehow, and send them with Joan. I was hoping that was all God wanted, although I knew better. I asked my husband to pray and believe that he would hear from the Lord on this. He agreed.

Two days later, Joan was here in Seattle ministering with me at a conference when I got a call from Jerry. He said he had heard from the Lord that I should go to Haiti. It was not an audible voice, a dream, or a vision. He just knew it on the inside and stated that more confirmation had just come in the mail.

Over the phone he began reading the Hallmark card that had come in the mail that day. On the inside was a handwritten prophetic word about the many lives that would be touched while I was in Haiti! Enclosed was a check for $1,000 with a heart-shaped sticky note attached that read, "This is one of *many* seeds that will come in; watch and see." The young lady who sent the card said she couldn't go in person, but would be there in spirit. She had been praying because I had shared the dreams, asking for agreement in prayer for divine orchestration over getting the prints mass produced and delivered to Haiti. Well, God showed her that I would actually be going myself! God gave her a word, and she followed through. God showed up in a huge way! Now, out of her obedience, God will bless her beyond measure, and I am so excited for her! It will be fun to see what God will do.

This extra trip was hard to fathom because I will also be going to Haiti by cruise ship in May when I host the "Heaven Touching Earth" Conference at Sea. But I was obedient and began planning, fasting, praying, and getting my shots. His ways are higher than my ways, and I would go full of the joy of the Lord. For years I had camped in rugged conditions, sleeping out in the open air or in a tent in the middle of nowhere by myself, hiking, hunting, and fishing, and I have taught others survival in the wilderness. God must know I can handle it, although it hasn't been on the top of my list of fun things to do in this season of my life. I am in total shock and awe of God in every aspect—first the dreams, then the invitation, then the checks in the mail, and everything else fell into place!

Jesus Smiling

I had absolutely no idea what to expect when arriving in Haiti. The television news captured the devastation from the perspective of media coverage, but to actually behold the destruction was beyond anything I have ever experienced. You see, each and every day, I ask the Lord to let me see through His eyes, hear through His ears, and feel through His heart, claiming every attribute of His character in everything I do and say as I go about my day. I bind my mind to the mind of Christ, holding the blood of Jesus against my own mind, will, and emotions. I ask the Lord to magnify the sensitivity of my spirit so I can see and hear directly from Him and respond promptly to His voice. *Help me, Lord, to surrender as close as possible to the magnitude that You surrendered to the Father as You walked the face of the earth so that I may carry out Your work here on earth.* That is how I always begin every day.

I wanted the people of Haiti to know that God hears their heart's cry, but everywhere I turned, there was death, sorrow, and darkness. I was feeling their pain and grief, but I began to smile. Now that may sound odd, but as quick and as deep as I felt their pain, suddenly, I would get a glimpse of Jesus smiling with sparkling, twinkling eyes. He has smiling eyes! I saw Him nodding His head and saying, "I have them. Trust Me, just trust Me. They will know I hear their heart's cry." I knew He would accomplish much through us just by His Love. I captured the vision of His love and glory bleeding off of us like a vapor. He said, "You are My glory containers, glory carriers, and glory dispensers; just love on My people and watch Me move."

Distributing the Prints

Nearly 10,000 prints of my Jesus painting were passed out among the people throughout the week. Thank God for the sensitivity in my spirit because if I would have listened to people telling me to at least put my website on the backs of the prints, I would have totally messed up God's plans for the people of Haiti. We were bundling up the prints to take out with us that first day when I heard Pastor Rene say, "I sure hope there isn't any information on them on where you could be tracked down because otherwise we can't let you give them out!" Praise God! I had followed divine orders from headquarters! Not even my signature was on them—no way to identify me, just Jesus! I was *so* happy, and what was about to happen brought me to my knees in awestruck tears of joy.

The people would reach out for a Jesus print like it was a piece of bread and they hadn't eaten in months. The facial expressions on the men, women, and children as they gazed at Jesus brought tears to my eyes. So many would just stare at the picture, either cry or smile, and then just place it over their eyes with both hands and rock back and forth. Some would place it on their hearts for a bit and then look at it again before placing it back on their hearts.

Each person was personally being ministered to by the Holy Spirit. The children would have ear-to-ear grins and just want to dance. We had so much fun dancing with the children and Jesus!

None Left Sick

Each of the three days of the healing crusade, the anointing grew as hundreds of thousands of people witnessed God's love through miracles, signs, and wonders. I am refilled and refueled typing this six weeks later! Easter night was the biggest explosion of healing that I have ever seen—from the woman who was healed when God's love melted her pain away and restored her arm, to the blind and deaf men and woman receiving back their sight and hearing instantly!

The first man was blind in both eyes, and when I praying the exact same prayer I had prayed for everyone that night, he received full sight! They brought me a second man who was blind in one eye and was in a lot of pain. Instantly the pain left and his vision was perfect. The crowd pressed in and I lost my transla- tor so two security officers followed me for the remainder of the night, keeping people back, but everybody was moving in and touching me and my clothes.

They would tap me and point to what was wrong. One of those taps was from a woman who brought a man who was deaf in one ear and a woman who was completely deaf in both ears. I prayed the same prayer and instantly they could hear. First the man and then the woman! The expression on her face, the screams, the jumping and twirling, and the excitement in the crowd over what Jesus had just done, will never leave me.

I stand in awe of my King who heals those who dare to believe. I have been in the healing ministry since 2000, but never have I experienced hundreds upon hundreds of healings, one right after another. Not one person turned away sick! I didn't have to tell them to keep believing or stay expectant because each and every one was instantly healed! The simple prayer the Lord had given me for each and every person was, "In the name of Jesus Christ, I curse the trauma off your body. I curse the trauma off your life. I command the pain to go and the healing virtue of Jesus Christ to flow into all that you are from the crown of your head to the soles of your feet. Body, heart, spirit, mind, and soul made whole, perfect, 100 percent complete. In Jesus' name, be healed." That was it! There were so many people that I told the translator not to repeat my prayer, but to just ask them what was wrong. I would pray, and then ask them how they felt. The excitement in their eyes was amazing as we shared the moment together. I can still hear them shouting the name of Jesus through their tears of joy! To God be *all* the glory, honor, and praise!

What a Treasure

Now that I am home, I miss everyone on the team immensely! What a treasure I found in my new friends. I believe we are forever fused together with Him and with each other. His love, compassion, peace, and joy operated through each and every one of us throughout the entire trip, bringing us into a position to deliver what God had for the people of Haiti. They knew God heard their heart's cry, and we all saw so many salvations, deliverances, healing miracles, signs, and wonders—each night escalating into a higher anticipation and greater expectation for more! God fed the hungry people of Haiti with the manifest presence of the Holy Spirit moving and operating through all of us.

CONCLUSION

Returning home to the U.S. after the amazing move of God we experienced in Haiti was a surreal experience. We all knew that God had allowed us to be a part of one of the biggest moves of His Spirit that Haiti had ever seen and that He intends our ministry there to be the first step in the rebuilding of an entire nation on a new foundation. We believe we shifted the spiritual foundations of the island as much as the earthquake moved the earth itself. We believe God wants to bring revival to the island that will transform it from a poor, corrupt, occult-riddled country to a prosperous, healthy, godly nation. We believe God intends to replace the current political structure with a new group of men who are known for their integrity. Not only are we praying for these changes, but we are also actively involving ourselves in various efforts toward restoration and transformation.

As has been mentioned throughout the book, Joan Hunter Ministries feels called to an ongoing connection to and ministry in Haiti. Already two cement trucks have been donated for Pastor Rene's rebuilding programs and are currently being prepared to ship to Haiti. We are also actively involved with plans for water filtration systems to be built and implemented at several locations on the island. God has allowed us to make contact with companies who have desalinization projects (making salt water safe to drink) and equipment for providing safe water for Haitians. We are also working with other ministries and companies in community development projects such as housing, agriculture, economic planning, schools, orphanages, job development, and financial stability for self-contained communities.

Right now in Haiti, there is a huge opportunity for God's people to use the resources that are in Haiti (mainly its people) along with modern technology and experience to continue to rebuild the nation. Christian people have a great opportunity to reach out and work alongside the Haitian government to see the country step into its God-ordained role as the Pearl of the Caribbean. We are so thankful for the part that God has called us to play in His incredible plans for Haiti.

Father God, I thank You for releasing Your concern for Haiti and the world into the hearts and minds of all those who read this book. May we be moved by the same things that move You. Empower us anew to release Your love and healing power around the world. Enlarge Your Kingdom rule and glorify Your name though Your people as You reign in our hearts. Father, let us be sensitive to Your leading to go where You have called us to go.

Amen!

Joan Hunter Ministries
Hearts 4 Him
4 Corners Healing and Conference Center

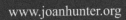

www.joanhunter.org

Equipping believers to take the healing power of God beyond the 4 walls of the church to the 4 corners of the earth.

Joan Hunter is a compassionate minister, dynamic teacher, an accomplished author, and an anointed healing evangelist. She has devoted her life to carry the message of hope, deliverance, and healing to the nations. As president and founder of Joan Hunter Ministries, Hearts 4 Him, and 4 Corners Healing and Conference Center, her vision is to **equip believers to take the healing power of God beyond the 4 walls of the church to the 4 corners of the earth.**

Joan ministers the Gospel with manifestations of supernatural signs and wonders in healing encounters, healing schools, miracle services, conferences, churches, and revival centers around the world. She leads the Worldwide Day of Healing that she and her parents started in 2005. Being sensitive to the move of the Spirit, Joan speaks prophetically in the services corporately, as well as releasing personal prophetic ministry to those in attendance. Joan's genuine approach and candid delivery enables her to connect intimately with people from all educational, social, and cultural backgrounds. Some have described her as being like Carol Burnett with the anointing of Jesus, because of her sense of humor.

Joan Hunter brings a powerful ministry to a world characterized by brokenness and pain. Having emerged victorious through tragic circumstances, impossible obstacles, and immeasurable devastation, Joan shares a message of hope and restoration to the broken hearted, deliverance and freedom to the bound, and healing and wholeness to the diseased. Joan's life is one of uncompromising dedication to the Gospel of Jesus Christ, and she exhibits a sincere desire to see the Body of Christ live free, happy, and whole.

Joan committed her life to Christ at the tender age of 12 and began faithfully serving in His Kingdom. She has served in ministry alongside her parents, Charles and Frances Hunter, as they traveled around the globe ministering in healing schools, miracle services, and healing explosions. Prior to branching out into her own International Healing Ministry, Joan co-pastored a church for 18 years.

Joan has authored five books: *Healing the Whole Man Handbook, Healing the Heart, Power to Heal, Endtime Economics and Healings, Miracles and Supernatural Experiences. Healing the Whole Man Handbook* is an exhaustive guide for physical healing, providing key insights into the root causes of hundreds of diseases with step-by-step instructions about how to pray specifically for each. *Healing the Heart* is Joan's personal testimony of going from brokenness to wholeness, providing timeless insight for overcoming impossible situations. *Power to Heal* is about how to gain freedom from oppression, overcome the past, learn keys to true forgiveness, unblock your healing, break the cycles of dependency, break generational curses, and break the devil's authority all in one book. *Endtime Economics* releases the financial breakthrough into the Body of Christ and is a must read in these end times. *Healings, Miracles and Supernatural Experiences* includes 36 life-changing testimonies of people who went to Haiti and ministered to the nation after the earthquake in April 2010. It tells of their obedience and how God moved in their lives before, during, and after the journey.

Joan has ministered in miracle services and conducted healing schools in numerous countries including: the United States, Haiti, El Salvador, Hong Kong, New Zealand, the Republic of the Philippines, Brazil, Columbia, Guatemala, Australia, Canada, Northern Ireland, The Republic of Ireland, Israel, England, Mexico, Peru, Singapore, Japan, and the Ukraine. She has also had numerous television and radio appearances including Sid Roth's "It's Supernatural," "It's a New Day," "The Miracle Channel," Steve Shultz's "Prophetic TV," and many others. Joan's television appearances have been broadcast around the world on World Harvest Network, Inspiration Network, Daystar, Faith TV, Cornerstone TV, The Church Channel, Extreme Prophetic with Patricia King, Total Christian Television, Christian Television Network, Watchmen Broadcasting, Today with Marilyn (Hickey) and Sarah, and God TV.

Joan and her husband, Kelley, reside in Pinehurst, Texas (NW Houston). They have four daughters, four sons, and four

Booking Information
281-789-7500
admin@joanhunter.org

PO Box 777
Pinehurst, TX 77362-0777
281-789-7500 ♥ fax 281-789-7497

THE PROCEEDS OF THIS BOOK WILL
CONTINUE TO HELP HAITI

**If you would like to make a donation
specifically to help support Haiti,**

You may contact:

JOAN HUNTER MINISTIES

PO Box 777 • Pinehurst, TX 77362-0777
Office Ph. 281-789-7500 Fax 281-789-7497
www.joanhunter.org • © Joan Hunter Ministries

What is God calling you to do?

_____

_____

_____

_____

_____

_____

_____

_____

_____

_____

_____

_____

_____

_____

_____

_____

_____

_____

_____

What is God calling you to do?

What is God calling you to do?

What is God calling you to do?

_____

_____

_____

_____

_____

_____

_____

_____

_____

_____

_____

_____

_____

_____

_____

_____

_____

_____

What is God calling you to do?

What is God calling you to do?

_____

_____

_____

_____

_____

_____

_____

_____

_____

_____

_____

_____

_____

_____

_____

_____

_____

_____

What is God calling you to do?

_____

_____

_____

_____

_____

_____

_____

_____

_____

_____

_____

_____

_____

_____

_____

_____

_____

_____

What is God calling you to do?

_____

_____

_____

_____

_____

_____

_____

_____

_____

_____

_____

_____

_____

_____

_____

_____

_____

In the right hands This Book will Change Lives!

Most of the people that need this message will not be looking for this book. To change their life you need to put a copy of this book in their hands.

> *But others (seeds) fell into good ground, and brought forth fruit, some a hundred-fold, some sixty-fold, some thirty-fold* (Matthew 13:3-8).

Our ministry is constantly seeking methods to find the good ground, the people that need this anointed message to change their life. Will you help us reach these people?

> *Remember this—a farmer who plants only a few seeds will get a small crop. But the one who plants generously will get a generous crop* (2 Corinthians 9:6).

EXTEND THIS MINISTRY BY SOWING
3-BOOKS, 5-BOOKS, 10-BOOKS, OR MORE TODAY,
AND BECOME A LIFE CHANGER!

Thank you,

Don Nori Sr., Publisher
Destiny Image
Since 1982